PRAISE FOR *MOMENTS*

"*Moments: Meditations from My Heart* is an intimate, graceful look into the sources of inspiration of Gary Conrad, one of America's most original authors. Make his *Moments* part of your moments, and you'll be richly rewarded."

> Larry Dossey, M.D., author of *One Mind: How Our Individual Mind Is Part of a Greater Consciousness and Why It Matters.*

"Gary Conrad explores deeply felt emotions in this fine collection of short stories and poetry."

> Carolyn Hart, author of the Bailey Ruth series

"*Moments: Meditations from My Heart* is filled with heartwarming nuggets of life. There are so many memories, some full of sorrow, others of delight, all thoughtful, created in such diverse locales as Tibet, Oklahoma, Paris, London... Some bring tears, others a smile or an out-loud laugh. *Moments* is a book to savor."

> Joan Korenblit, Respect Diversity Foundation

"Hold on tight and brace yourself as author Gary Conrad transports you into his sometimes hair-raising and electrifying world. I held my breath with him when he was caught in a whirlpool that dragged him to the bottom of a turbulent river, I tightly gripped the book for balance as he shakily trekked near the edge of a precipitous cliff, I cried as he told a devastated family about the death of a loved one, and yet he also shared the pleasure of quiet, serendipitous moments. His honesty, transparency, vulnerability, and optimism are captivating and refreshing. Each short journey into Gary's adventures is like taking a world tour from an easy chair."

> Sue Tarr, author, educator, and passionate
> organic farmer

"Gary Conrad's newest book made me laugh, smile, cry, think, and ponder. *Moments* is a book to savor. Conrad obviously knows and cares about what is truly important. He seeks to live his life mindful of the power of kindness, the holiness of relationship, the joy of serving, the grace of forgiveness. This book is a keeper–one to which I shall return often for inspiration."

> Dr. Roberta Damon, author of *A Voice Beyond
> Weeping*

MOMENTS

Meditations from My Heart

GARY D. CONRAD

Published by Ahimsa Press
3126 S. Boulevard St., #285
Edmond, OK 73013
Website: GaryDConrad.com

Cover image from iStock:
Sunrise at Haleakala National Park, Maui, Hawaii
Author photo: Chris Corbett
Cover design: Steve Boaldin
Interior design: Marilyn Ratzlaff

Written, Printed and Produced in the United States of America

To Thich Nhat Hanh
Master of the present moment
Master of mindfulness
Master of life

Contents

1. Another Day in Paradise   1
2. A Bird's Life   7
3. Thunderstorms   11
4. Little Bug   14
5. Monte Sol   16
6. What Really Matters   19
7. Not Enough Air   24
8. Someday   30
9. India   32
10. Chopping Cotton   37
11. Glowworms   40
12. As Above, So Below   44
13. A Moment in Time   45
14. When I am Gone   47
15. The Son I Never Knew   49
16. Smartphones, Tools, or Traps?   51
17. His Eye Is on the Sparrow   55
18. Wind Chimes   60
19. Texting   63
20. Fear   65
21. An Ocean of Wildflowers   72
22. Aging   76
23. Roadkill   81

24. Autumn   83
25. Sleeping In as a Spiritual Practice   87
26. Dancers   90
27. God   94
28. Love Never Dies   96
29. Healing Touch   101
30. Damn the Torpedoes   103
31. Searching for God   106
32. The Wart   108
33. The Leader of the Band   114
34. The Chocolate Chip Cookie   119
35. The Time Portal   122
36. Guilt   130
37. Springtime   133
38. Memories of a Distant Time   134
39. Rain   141
40. Deafening   144
41. Miraculous   149

Introduction

The Ancient Greeks gave us two concepts as ways to think about and to employ time: *kronos* and *kairos*. *Kronos* measures time in a successive order of events to become chronology which provides a narrative. *Kronos* is the time of calendars and clocks. *Kairos,* translated as an "opportune moment" or "right time," recounts an event that creates a crucial action, a moment that remains imprinted in memory that we can revisit and relive as a freestanding event. A personal example of *kairos* occurs when I smell the fragrance of Old Spice, a favorite of my grandfather, Harold Conrad. As I breathe in the familiar, comforting scent, I am transported to a place of love, my grandparents' farm near Friendship, Oklahoma. My mind is flooded with pleasant memories of tractor rides, fabulous meals, overalls, warm family gatherings, and swimming in a farm pond that was, in truth, an oversized red dirt mud-hole.

After composing *The Pit*, I originally thought that I would write a sequel to my first book, *The Lhasa Trilogy.* I started with gusto, with *kronos*, developing a writing plan, a narrative of the first few chapters, excited to be starting on a new project. Then I realized I was being pulled in a different direction, and I felt the need to contrast the stark, somewhat harsh, painful reality of *The Pit* with something gentler, with words that echo from my heart and head.

And so, *Moments: Meditations from My Heart* was spawned by means of *kairos*, random memory reconnections that revealed themselves to me with the momentary recall of emotion and feeling. As a disclaimer, please know that portions of the book have been carefully selected from the best of my previous writings over the years, but none from my published books. Most will be fresh and new, and I hope these compositions resonate with you. To satisfy those who enjoyed *The Pit*, there will also be a smattering of real-life medical tales, along with their associated intensity. The book, though, whether in poetry or in short story form, will focus on intimate, unique moments in my life, coupled with the microscope of mindfulness. In this book, the reader will have a lingering peek at my open heart and soul, which I gladly share.

Thank you for walking this path with me.

Moments

What is life but moments?
Fleeting seconds that come and go
Never to be seen again.
Moments become minutes,
Minutes – hours,
Hours – days,
Days – years,
Years – a lifetime.
Hold them as we may,
We cannot.
Moments pass before us
Like sand in an hourglass,
Inexorable.
Yet, if we hold each as sacred,
We can savor each and every one
Fully aware,
Fully conscious,
Knowing them for what they truly are,
The sum of our lives.

– Gary D. Conrad

Chapter One

ANOTHER DAY IN PARADISE

In 1978, as a fledgling emergency physician, I worked with a cadre of experienced nurses who guided me through the confusing maze of a busy emergency department. One of the RNs I worked with was Rick, a seasoned, skilled nurse who could be relied on in the most challenging of situations. Tall and slender with piercing brown eyes, he had a pale complexion and straight dark-brown hair with a matching moustache. When I walked through the doors of the emergency department and saw him sitting at the desk, I would ask, "Hey Rick, how's it going?"

Almost invariably, with an emotionless stare on his face, he'd reply, "Another day in paradise."

My initial reaction to his cynical quip was one of disbelief. After all, in this setting we had the opportunity to do enormous good for others, and not only that, we were well paid for our efforts. As a result, we had food, comfortable homes, and the financial means to enjoy our lives.

But the longer I labored in "The Pit," the more I realized how often we caregivers were placed in situations that shook us to the core of our beings. The emergency department was not a Disney movie, and happy endings did not always occur. In retrospect, I came to understand that Rick was not a cynic, but rather, a realist. He saw the events of life for what they were, not for what he hoped they would be. He didn't believe that when he had lemons, he made lemonade, as the cliché goes. He just had lemons. All those years ago, he pulled off my rose-colored glasses and made me see the world as it really was. Without realizing it, Rick was preparing me for the greatest healthcare challenge that I or any of us in medicine would ever face.

∞∞∞

Never, during my forty-two years in the emergency department have I experienced anything like the coronavirus pandemic. No one has. The acuity, mayhem and need for quick action are higher than I've ever seen.

One of the main reasons for the pandemonium is that people are delaying necessary medical treatment, fearful they will become infected by the coronavirus while at the hospital. And so, they stay at home, becoming sicker and sicker, and finally, by the time they realize they need to be seen by a physician, it's too late. When EMS arrives at the scene, they may either be dead or close to it. If they are alive when they arrive at the emergency department, it's all hands on deck to save them.

Another cause for such criticality is the nature of the coronavirus itself. To date in Oklahoma, we have already had over 204,000 cases with 1,834 deaths. As bad as these numbers are in the general population, the virus is much more devastating in vulnerable groups, such as those with diabetes, asthma, chronic obstructive pulmonary disease (COPD), autoimmune diseases, and the elderly, especially those who reside in assisted living or nursing home facilities. In those locations, once the virus gains access, it spreads like a raging wildfire through a dry, summertime California forest. I've never seen more severely ill patients than these people, and a number require emergent intubation to keep them alive.

Because of the nurse shortage and the incredible volume of sick patients, the hospital is often packed to capacity, leading to an overflow of admitted patients who have to stay in the emergency department until a bed becomes available. Given the scarcity of open beds statewide, the physician is in La La Land if he believes a transfer of the patient to another facility is possible.

Due to the overcrowding, the nurses not only have to care for emergency patients, suffering from heart attacks, strokes, broken bones and such, but now also those sickened by the coronavirus. In the meantime, if the patient's condition deteriorates while waiting to go upstairs to a room, the emergency physician has to intervene and do whatever is necessary, no matter that he or she has far too many others to attend to. Experienced nurses I have labored with for decades have told me how physically, emotionally, and mentally beaten down they are, but they are no exception. After months of intense pressure, we are *all* exhausted, from the nurses, doctors, EMTs, paramedics, x-ray technicians, to laboratory personnel. The vaccine gives us hope, but can we hang on by our fingernails, gritting our teeth until its effect is seen in the months ahead?

It's not in the DNA of emergency personnel to complain. We just don't. We are a tough, hardy lot, who can take just about anything and do whatever is necessary. That said, certain aspects of the pandemic are taking a toll on me, tarnishing the shiny veneer of my occupation as an emergency physician.

First of all, I'm tired of seeing so many of my fellow Oklahomans suffocate and die from the coronavirus. These are not just numbers put out by the CDC, they are grandparents, fathers, mothers, and children, real people who are greatly loved, and their loss creates a vacuum that can never be filled. And though it's not nearly as bad as having Covid-19, I'm emotionally drained by repeatedly telling families that their loved ones have passed away. And if the patient is dying, I'm the bearer of the news that it's too dangerous to let the family say their goodbyes in person. Risk or no risk, my heart and soul scream at the inhumanity of what we are required to do in the best interests of the family.

I'm tired of dreading going to work and wondering about what I might face. *Will this be the patient from whom I'll contract this sometimes fatal disease?* I'm sixty-eight and in a high-risk population myself. Never have I had to be this concerned about becoming ill and possibly dying as a consequence of doing my job.

I'm tired of wondering as I'm en route to the emergency department: *Is this the day I will be presented with more than I can handle? How many will die today? Will I have a moment to urinate? A few minutes for a snack, maybe?*

I'm tired of staying late, hours past the end of my shift to finish caring for the patients who are far too complex to hand off to colleagues, who, minutes after stepping into the emergency department, usually have their own chaos to manage. After work, I go home, strip off my clothes and take a long, hot shower. Then I limp upstairs to my office and stare blankly at the computer screen, barely seeing the images, trying to put aside the disquieting scenes of the day indelibly etched in my mind

I'm tired of worrying about whether I will infect my wife or my ninety-one year old father. *Am I an asymptomatic carrier?* Should either of them become ill or die because I carried the disease from the hospital to them, I would never be able to forgive myself.

I'm tired of looking at my hands, red, chapped, cracked, and sometimes bleeding, from being washed so often. Lotion only helps so much.

I'm tired of hearing paramedics encode the hospital with another nursing home patient who can't breathe. I have come to dread the distinctive ring of the ambulance phone, so often a harbinger of an incoming nightmare.

I'm tired of the ineffective leadership we have in Washington. Our President knew of the seriousness of the coronavirus in January of 2020, yet he blatantly lied and minimized the danger to the American public, and the steps he took to deal with the problem were inept and inadequate. No doubt the pandemic would have still happened, but not to the severity into which it has morphed. The Boston Globe has stated the obvious: President Trump has "blood on his hands."

∞∞∞∞

I confess that in spite of the gravity of our situation, I am an eternal optimist. I know that as Americans and world citizens, we will find a way to push through this, but not without residual scars. While I remain hopeful, each time I drive to work in the emergency department, I hear Rick's words echoing in my mind.

Another day in paradise?

In other words: Another day in Hell?

It will be; it's guaranteed. For all those caregivers who selflessly sacrifice themselves to help others, there is no escape. We keep going. We must.

There is no other option.

This chapter was first published in the January 2021 edition of The Oklahoma Observer.

Chapter Two

A BIRD'S LIFE

There are very few things in life I enjoy more than watching the airborne hustle and bustle of a bird feeder. Everything about the whole experience is unpredictable and meditative, and I find myself wondering: *What kind of birds will I see today? Will I get a glimpse of a species that I've never identified before? Will a spectacularly beautiful painted bunting finally make an appearance?*

As I sit and gaze at the birds flying in and out, I imagine how great it would be to have the carefree existence of a bird. At first glance, one would believe that a bird's life would be like the metaphoric easy street. Think about it. Their primary duties are to soar and pirouette as high in the sky as they can reach, eat from the abundant harvest of nature and sing their melodies. That doesn't sound like too rough of a life, does it?

But the more I think about it, the more I realize that other, more challenging obligations are required of our fine-feathered friends. After the singing, mating rituals, and

displays of virility by the males, which bind the loving couple together like an avian Sonny and Cher, the natural urge
for coupling occurs, which eventually leads to nest building,
a clutch of little speckled eggs, and the duties of parenthood.
Once hatched, typically mom stays home and watches after
her squirming, demanding hatchlings, while dad continu-
ously forages in the wild to bring back food. Not exactly a
walk in the park.

And how would you feel if each time you returned to
your humble twig abode, everyone was screaming at you,
demanding something to eat? I can almost hear the com-
plaints: "I'm tired of worms; can't you find something else for
a change? The ladybug looks too cute to eat. Can I play with
her? What are we having for dessert?" There is no rest for
the bedraggled parents, who have no winged therapist they
can go to for psychological help, even though they are likely
on the verge of complete insanity.

Besides, unless you made your nest as deep as the
Mariana Trench, the possibility exists that while Junior is
horseplaying with his brothers, Ollie and Waldo, he might
lose his balance, fall out of the nest, and be mortally wounded on the ground below. To your dismay, when he actually
does just that, in the blink of an eye, he is pounced on by the
neighborhood cat, Fuzzball, who had been sitting patiently
at the foot of the tree, smacking her lips and waiting for this
golden opportunity. As you fly down in desperation, you
discover that the wicked feline has her partially open, drool-
ing mouth full of your mangled chick, who somehow is able
to squeak out, "Daddy, please help me," just before he takes
his last breath.

How horrible is that?

What about the other vicious predators that are lurk-

ing in the shadows waiting for any opportunity to pounce
and disembowel you and your brood? Can you imagine
watching helplessly as your shapely, unsuspecting cardinal
wife, Edith, is plucked out of mid-air, kicking and screaming
by a vicious hawk? You stare in horror as you see her struggle
against the vise-like grip of his razor-sharp talons, brown-
ish-red feathers flying every which way. In moments, though,
she goes limp, lifelessly bobbing up and down with each flap
of the hawk's wings, just before she is carried off into the
deep blue sky, never to be seen again.

Yikes!

And consider owls, the stealthy raptors of the night.
How could you ever feel safe after sunset with those noc-
turnal hunters marauding at will from tree to tree, hoping
to find a plump, tasty bird for a nighttime snack? Can you
picture sitting in your wifeless nest, now that Edith is gone,
with your only two remaining chicks as company? You're
peacefully watching the full moon rising over the horizon after a hard day of foraging, when all of a sudden, two glowing,
dilated yellow eyes hover before you, scouring the area for
prey. You silently put your trembling wings over your nest-
lings' beaks and crouch down in the nest, praying to the Al-
mighty Bird God that they don't make a peep, flutter a feath-
er, tweet or move a muscle.

I shiver as I think about it.

As I emerge from my nightmarish daydream, I sigh in
relief as I discover that I am no longer living a bird's life. I
gaze up and see that the feeder is now flush with activity.
A red-bellied woodpecker, with his large orange cap, has
just made an appearance. Soon after he flies away, a blue jay
lands on a perch and, as the alpha bird, takes control of the
feeder. Little chickadees deftly flit in and out from the adja-

cent landing, trusting that they will be able to avoid the jay's clumsy pecks.

Come to think of it, perhaps I can soar, pirouette . . . well, maybe not pirouette . . . eat heartily and sing my song, without being a bird.

Certainly seems safer that way, doesn't it?

Chapter Three

THUNDERSTORMS

As I lay in bed on an early June morning, I woke to the symphonic reverberation of rolling thunder. Knowing that sleep was now finished, I turned from my side to my back, tucked my pillow under my head and enjoyed the cacophony of sounds as they echoed into the bedroom, my home rattling ever-so-slightly with each booming thunderclap. I'm not sure why, but there's something about thunderstorms that makes me feel alive and vibrant. Perhaps it's the thrill of experiencing the uninhibited power of nature, or maybe it's the edgy anticipation of how piercingly loud the next rumble might be. *Will the splitting crack of a nearby bolt of lightning be next?*

Several years ago, when I was solo hiking in Canyonlands National Park in Utah, seemingly from nowhere, the baddest-of-the-bad high-desert thunderstorms crept up on me from behind, like a cloaked, silent stalker, evil on his mind. Suddenly, brilliant, scintillating streaks of lightning exploded all around me – far too close for comfort – followed by torrential rain. Terrified beyond my wildest imagination and hoping not to be fried to a crisp like those cartoon characters whose skeletons are briefly lit up when they are electrocuted, I frantically surveyed the area and discovered a rock overhang under which I took refuge. Now feeling safe, I could almost picture the magnificent Zeus standing tall on top of a thunderhead with his flowing grey beard, laughing as I cowered from the lightning bolts he'd flung in my direction.

After the storm moved on, I experienced the soft, fragrant aroma of clean, negative ion-enriched air, but I also felt a bit of sadness. While I was grateful to be alive, the excitement and its associated adrenaline rush had gone.

When I think of the power of nature, I recall an incident that occurred when my wife Sheridan and I were visiting Tibet in 2008. We had gone there so that I might gather information for the composition of *The Lhasa Trilogy*. While we were exploring the capital city of Lhasa, a powerful earthquake hit, violently shaking the city for a few moments. Once we got our wits about us, and we no longer feared seeing the earth open up before us and our toppling into a gaping, miles-deep chasm, the guide informed us that the common folk believed when an earthquake occurred, it signified the birth of a spiritual being, perhaps a high lama, into Tibet. Given the brutal and repressive Chinese government currently in power, the Tibetans certainly need all the help they can get to confront their challenges.

Now, as I sit and contemplate this notion, I realize our country has its own set of difficult, seemingly overwhelming issues, and the idea occurs to me that perhaps we would benefit from our own, unique American metaphor for the Tibetan earthquake. I am keen on the concept that the lightning bolt, with all its visceral, untamed power, announces the birth, not of an advanced soul, but of fresh viewpoints, ones that have the potential to promote change for good.

Since that blustery June morning, I've altered my way of thinking about thunderstorms. The next time I hear one rumbling overhead, I'm going to imagine that the jolting thunder and lightning are doing their best to shake me up and prod me into new understandings. Deep within myself, I know, if I change how I think, I can change myself, and if I change myself, I can do my part to change our country and even the world. Probably not in grand ways, but more likely in small ones. Mother Teresa once said, "Not all of us can do great things. But we can do small things with great love."

Amen to that.

Thunderstorm, anyone?

Chapter Four

LITTLE BUG

Tiny insect on the floor
Watching as I notice you,
Small and brown,
Trembling?
I wonder what you think of me.
A lumbering, hulking giant
Who, without a second thought
Could painfully end your life,
Crushing you with a shoe?
A tissue?
A fly swatter?
Maybe you know of others
Who have died in such a way,
Or perhaps were crippled,
Escaping to die later,
A slow, lingering death.
Now here you are
Confronted with your own mortality.

You wonder
What will the monster do?
Reading its thoughts, I silently say:
Little bug,
You have nothing to fear from me.
I respect the life within you
As you respect mine.
All life is sacred,
No matter how big,
No matter how small.
I have no wish for you to suffer
Or to prematurely end your life.
We can share this space together.
We can coexist.
Rest easy.
I love you.

Chapter Five

Monte Sol

Santa Fe, New Mexico, is a place of magic, a location where one is enveloped by a unique amalgam of spirit and matter, oozing with the energy of the Divine. My wife, Sheridan, and I have made it a habit to visit yearly to see Amma, also known as the "Hugging Saint," to receive *darshan,* a blessing, through her holy embrace.

Besides this sacred event, Santa Fe also has an incredible array of restaurants, art, and trekking to enjoy. We had hiked trails at two nearby national monuments, Bandelier, a land of canyons and plateaus that harbor ruins of the Ancient Puebloans, and Kasha-Katuwe Tent Rocks, where one can wander among eons-old layers of volcanic rock eroded by wind and weather into strange, otherworldly conical formations.

This year, though, we wanted to explore somewhere different. Our friend Judge, one of the proprietors of Ravens Ridge Bed and Breakfast, suggested the Monte Sol Trail, also called the Sun Mountain Trail, located directly off the Old Santa Fe Trail Highway. By car, the trail was a mere five minutes from our lodgings. On the surface, the hike didn't appear to be too challenging. Judge estimated that this two-mile trek would take a total of two hours up and down, and the elevation change was a manageable eight hundred sixty feet. So, ready to taste the wilderness, we drove to the trailhead, parked our vehicle, and set off to experience the mystery of nature.

Before long, we realized that this hike was not for the weak of heart. After about a hundred yards of a gradual incline, we hit a series of switchbacks that ascended a steep slope seemingly straight up the mountain. Every step had to be measured carefully, as the loose scree made the placement of our boots critically important. We had to pause more often than I care to confess to give our heart rates a chance to fall below one hundred and sixty beats a minute. Shortly, my clothes were soaked with sweat as the intense New Mexico sun relentlessly beat down on us.

But yet, even in the midst of the intense physical challenge, I noticed various multicolored desert flowers – yellows, whites, reds, and purples – arising from cracks in the rocky surfaces, as if to tell me that despite the challenges of life, beauty can spring forth from desolation. Butterflies flitted around us, mostly variations of blacks and whites, demonstrating the importance of finding joy in every moment. Ravens circled overhead, silently scanning the landscape for a tasty meal of carrion, rodents, or bird eggs. Small brown lizards darted across our path, disappearing as quickly as they arrived, their earth-tone colorings camouflaging them from our eyes. Many small groupings of holes in the earth were the burrows of cicadas, a harbinger of things to come.

After a little over an hour, Sheridan and I breathlessly arrived at the summit of Monte Sol and gazed at the beautiful adobe city of Santa Fe spread out below us. We felt not only the continued intensity of the sun, but also forceful gusts of wind that threatened to blow us off our feet. Seeking shelter from the elements, Sheridan discovered a gnarled, low-hanging piñon pine tree that provided a welcome measure of shade over some large rocks suitable for sitting. Bending over to enter the small, cocoon-like space, we sat down, feeling branches gently brushing up against us. After a snack of tasty milk chocolate with hazelnuts, we both lay down on a soft bed of pine needles, watching the sun peek through the tree limbs. As I closed my eyes, I could hear the comforting rhythmic humming sound of cicadas, along with the occasional buzzing of flies.

As I rested, I realized that the cicadas were Mother Nature's symphony, with the flies sounding much like off-key violins. The blustery wind was the cooling breath of God, and the sun Her guiding light, while the enveloping tree was as a Divine womb. I felt safe, nurtured, and peaceful. Other hikers wandered into the area, but I paid no attention to their idle banter. Nothing could penetrate the sacred space I had entered.

Sometime later, Sheridan and I emerged from our arboreal sanctuary, refreshed and relaxed. After a few final moments at the summit, we patiently hiked back down the mountain, mindfully placing each step. In the afternoon light, we noticed many shining pieces of mica on and alongside the trail. I felt as if I were dancing among the stars of a faraway galaxy, and who knows, maybe I was.

Arriving back at the trailhead, we shed our backpacks, stowed them in our car, and drove away, knowing that in the hours to come, we would enter Amma's presence, guaranteed to be a profound spiritual experience.

Two blessed happenings in one day?

My cup overflowed with joy and gratitude.

Chapter Six

WHAT REALLY MATTERS

"People suffer because they are caught in their views. As soon as we release those views, we are free and we don't suffer anymore."

– Thich Nhat Hanh

On occasion, I find myself feeling passionate about specific thoughts or activities that are not important, and because of this, as Thich Nhat Hanh has said, I suffer. With this in mind, in the hope of saving time and energy in the future, I've put together a list of things that I consider to be of little consequence, and another of items that I believe to be worthwhile. As you read my compilations, you might take a few moments to consider, "What comprises my lists? What is important (and unimportant) to me? In which areas do I want to focus my attention, and where would I prefer to spend less time?"

Now, as Jackie Gleason might say, "And away we go!"

19

What doesn't matter:

    1. *Sporting events.* I can't believe I've put this at the top of the list. I love watching the Oklahoma City Thunder, and many a nail-biting evening I've sat with my father and son-in-law, screaming at the top of my lungs, trying to cheer Big Blue on to a win. But, at the end of the day, while I enjoy these times and the camaraderie immensely, it's rare for the games, in and of themselves, to have any important long-term effect in the world.

    2. *Constantly wearing the latest fashions.* Unless it's required for one's employment, how worthless is this? It's as if someone is saying: *Look at me! Can't you see how hip and up-to-date I am?*

    3. *What others think about me.* If I live a life where I stand up for what I believe, some folks will like me, others won't, and that's just fine with me.

    4. *A lavish lifestyle.* While enjoying the finer things in life on occasion is undoubtedly pleasurable, it's hard to justify a constant stream of overabundance and endless consumption of material goods when so many in the world are starving, thirsty, diseased, and barely able to survive.

    5. *Cosmetic procedures.* Facelifts, Botox injections, liposuction, hair transplants, and other vanity-based procedures performed to preserve the illusion of eternal youth are a waste of time. Contrary to what we've been conditioned to believe in our Western culture, generally appearance is *not* everything. I've heard on occasion that if such alterations in the way we look make us feel better about ourselves, how can that be bad? Well, I suppose it all depends on one's perspective. My Buddhist friends would ask, knowing we will all die someday, does it really matter

if we look good just before we begin to molder in the grave?

What does matter:

1. *Kindness.* The Dalai Lama once said, "My religion is kindness." Deservedly this quality stands at the beginning of the list.

2. *Raising children in a loving, caring manner.* I've repeatedly said that the most important thing I have done this lifetime is to help raise my three daughters. They are truly the living legacy of my life.

3. *Butterflies.* What better excmplifies a joyful existence than these beautiful, innocent insects that flit and dance through the sky for no other reason than to express their love of life?

4. *Mindfulness.* The past is over, the future is yet to be, and all one has is the present moment. Live it in full awareness.

5. *Laughter.* A good guffaw has been described as the "best medicine," and I couldn't agree more.

6. *Meditation.* Few things are more worthwhile than probing the Universe that exists within and without.

7. *Helping others.* Preferably, assistance should be given in a way that allows those in need to help themselves. Donating to charities is certainly a grand deed, but giving in a manner that promotes self-empowerment is even better.

8. *Eating a healthy diet/exercise.* The apostle Paul once said, "Do you not know that your body is a temple of the Holy Spirit? Therefore honor God with your body." In other words, how can you perform your soul's work if your body is not cared for properly and suffers the unfortunate consequences?

9. *Awareness of what is occurring in the world.* Here, a balance is necessary. While being informed is important, on occasion I have to take a news fast and withdraw from the troubling happenings of our Earth. Otherwise, I'll find myself continually mired in a state of dismay about tragic events over which I have little or no control.

10. *Sunrises and sunsets.* To see the Technicolor glory of God in the morning and evening is always a blessing.

11. *The love and support of family and friends.* At times, life presents challenges that are difficult to handle on my own. Thank God for those whom I love and those who likewise care for me. I couldn't survive without these precious ones in my life.

12. *The environment.* We should do all that we can to preserve our world for generations to come. No soul-waiting-to-be-born should be incarnated into an overheated, polluted, cesspool of a planet.

13. *Trees.* I love connecting with the spiritual energy of these ancient spirits.

14. Anything that gives me that warm, tingly, joyful feeling in my heart.

With time and patience, my fervent wish increases that I'll learn to focus less on the first list and more on the second. Spiritual teachers would tell us that the seeds we water are the ones that will flourish. In other words, where I direct my attention is the place where the most growth will invariably occur, whether with activities that resonate as meaningful or with those that are insignificant or perhaps even harmful. All this said, I will not be a stickler about the happenings of my life, and flexibility, not rigidity, will always be my prime directive. I have no doubt that even so-called hard and fast rules are meant to be broken on occasion.

Saying all this, I must confess that I'll still whoop it up during Thunder games.

Chapter Seven

NOT ENOUGH AIR

Some moments in life are critical junctures, leading to totally different realities dependent on the outcomes. One such happening occurred to me many years ago, and even today, I shudder when I think about what could have taken place.

∞∞∞

After my divorce in 1992, I made it a habit to take my daughters on summer vacations to various locations in the Southwest, including Sedona, Santa Fe, Durango, and Ouray, familiar places that we all enjoyed immensely. Driving cross-country to these locations from Guthrie, Oklahoma, we listened and sang our hearts out to Neil Diamond as he sang our favorite family song, "Porcupine Pie," from his classic album, *Moods*.

In our travels, we ate lots of great food, hiked many wonderful trails, and just enjoyed spending time together.

Some events we repeated yearly, simply because they were guaranteed fun. Ouray, in southwest Colorado, "The Switzerland of America," was our favorite, even though the route to get there was a frightening experience, with twelve miles of hairpin turns that would make the traveler gasp in terror. Every so often, we would squirm and wonder: *Are we going off the edge?* The circuitous high-elevation stretch in the Rocky Mountains is known as the "Million Dollar Highway," and has been labeled by *USA Today* as one of the "World's Twelve Most Dangerous Roads."

After we survived the treacherous highway, we always ate breakfast the following morning at Cecilia's, where we treated ourselves to world-famous Golden Pancakes, emphasis on the word *Golden.* Then, we'd soak in the natural hot springs and later watch the Gary Davis Show, a medley of various country and pop songs, including an unforgettable Elvis impersonation that always made us tap our toes. And who of us could ever forget his version of the hilarious song, "I Lobster And Never Flounder?"

But before that, we always stopped in Durango for a day or two to take in a float trip of some sort on the nearby Animas River, where the challenging Smelter Rapids awaited us. Usually, we chose river rafting, and that was terrifying enough, but this time, we decided to stretch our wings, test our mettle, and instead try inflatable kayaks.

After a brief training session with our guide, we set out on what we hoped would be the adventure of a lifetime. The sky was bright blue, clear, and cloudless, and the crisp morning air greeted us as we skirted across the water. The sparkling day was gorgeous, as it often is in southwest Colorado. Nothing could go wrong on such a glorious day, could it?

The river was relatively low that year, and we had to keep to the center so that our kayaks would not get caught on rocks, which normally would not have been exposed in higher water. The guide led us along in single file, much as ducklings follow their mother. Daughters Hillary and Megan were close behind, with me bringing up the rear. For reasons I don't remember now, my oldest daughter, Sarah, was not with us this time. We happily kayaked along, though I must confess that I felt a bit nervous as we approached the Smelter Rapids, which even from a distance seemed much more frothy and turbulent than I recalled.

As the guide had explained to us at the onset, we were to carefully follow his path through the rapids. While he didn't go into detail about what might happen if we wandered off in another direction, it was self-explanatory that such would likely be risky.

Just when we were about to enter the foam of the rapids, my kayak got hung up on one of those dreaded high rocks, and it took me some moments to dislodge it. When I finally shook myself free, I saw that the guide had not noticed my predicament, and he and my daughters had already ventured through the treacherous section.

But where did they cross?

If I hadn't been nervous beforehand, I certainly was now. I waited for a moment, and still, the guide didn't look back to check on me. It was up to me, and only me, to select the proper route. For a few seconds, I studied the vectors of the flowing water, chutes through the rocky obstacles, the standing waves and vortices – so many choices, so little time.

Gulp. I felt my heart in my throat. I thought: *Was my will up to date?*

Okay, here goes nothing, I thought as I chose and

paddled into a narrow channel between the rocks ahead, one I believed to be the best of the possible alternatives. Almost instantly, I discovered that I'd made the wrong decision, as at the very moment I entered the rapids, I was abruptly catapulted from my kayak into the ice-cold water.

I fought hard against feelings of panic as I was immediately sucked beneath the surface and down to the bottom of the river by a powerful current. Fortunately, I had taken a breath, though not a deep one, before I submerged. To my dismay, I found myself circling deep in the turbulent water, bouncing off rocks resting on the river floor, and I realized that the reason I was propelled from the kayak was a dreaded river whirlpool.

An eternity seemed to pass, though it was likely only one to two minutes. Feeling an impending sense of doom, I realized I was not ascending out of the trap that ensnared me, and I began to feel breathless. With no small amount of difficulty, I pushed back the strong, instinctual urge to breathe, knowing I would only suck in water and likely drown.

I approached unconsciousness, though just when I thought my situation was hopeless, and that I would die in the river version of Davy Jones's Locker, the whirlpool just as quickly released me from its icy grip. The buoyant force of my life jacket finally pro-pelled me upward from what could have been a watery tomb. The instant I felt my head break the surface, I took a gasping breath of life-saving air. With the pos-sible exception of when I took my first breath at child-birth, the sweet relief of inhalation has never been surpassed at any time in my life. Death would come at some other time, and I was alive.

Thank God.

∞∞∞

The first thing I noticed when I bobbed to the top of the water was Hillary and Megan, waiting expectantly in their kayaks a bit further downstream, just beyond the rapids. I'll never forget the looks of fear on their little faces, which quickly morphed into ones of relief when they realized that their Dad had not drowned. The guide appeared to be in a state of shock, and I'm positive that he realized that he had made what could have been a fatal error, one that could have been easily prevented had he simply been more attentive.

I swam over to him, and as he helped me back into my kayak, which he had retrieved. He asked, "Are you okay?"

"Yes."

"Good," he said, without any expression of regret.

And that was all that was said. I felt the guide had learned from his mistake, and that was enough for me. I didn't need an apology. None of us get it right all the time.

That said, I promised myself that I would never again get on an inflatable kayak.

∞∞∞

Now, many years later, as I look back on this terrifying experience, I find myself thinking about what I would have missed had I died, and a kaleidoscope of thoughts and images cross my mind. First, I would have never seen my children, Sarah, Megan, and Hillary graduate from high school and watch as they experienced the ups and downs of their lives. I would have never had the joy of being a grandfather to their children, Connor, Taylor, Sydney, Olivia, and Sawyer.

I can't even imagine.

I would have never met and married my spiritual partner, Sheridan, and would not have sat down beside her in meditation at the Tibetan holy lake, Yamdrok-tso. Of course, I would not have known her two wonderful sons, William and Alex. I would not have been here when my mother died, and I wouldn't have been around to help care for my father.

Besides all this, I would have missed caring for patients for over twenty years, and what kind of impact would that have had? It is completely inconceivable to think that I never would have constructed books, ones that express my creative inspirations in a way that I had never had done before.

God knows that my life would have been far less rich had I passed from this life to the next on that fated day, but I didn't. I had so much more to experience and, in keeping with the theme of this book, many more sacred moments to cherish.

I am grateful beyond words.

Chapter Eight

SOMEDAY

Someday, I may be cold.
   But now, I have warm clothes and a comfortable
   home.

Someday, my vision may blur.
   But now, I see the azure blue of the sky, blades of
   lush green grass, and the soft glow of the
   morning sun.

Someday, I may be hungry.
   But now, I enjoy the taste of good food and the feeling of a full stomach.

Someday, I may lose my sense of smell.
   But now, I delight in the aroma of flowers and the
   fresh scent of air after a rain.

Someday, I may be alone.
>   But now, I treasure the softness of my wife's
>   body as we sleep together.

Someday, my hearing may leave me.
>   But now, I listen to the twitter of birds dancing
>   outside my window.

Someday, the pets I love will no longer be at my side.
>   But now, I value rubbing their furry heads and
>   seeing the love in their eyes.

Someday, my health will fail.
>   But now, I appreciate my wellness.

Someday, those I love will die.
>   But now, I hold each second with them as sacred.

Someday, no one of this earth will be aware that
>   I existed.
>   But now, many know me.

Someday, when I die, I will leave everything of the
>   Earth behind.
>   But now, I embrace my life.

In the present moment, someday does not exist.
Only the here and now.
And for that, I am grateful.

Chapter Nine

India

Is this love of mine blind sentiment
That sees not the pathways of reason?
Ah, no! I love India,
For there I learned first to love God
and all things beautiful.
Some teach to seize the fickle dewdrop, life,
Sliding down the lotus leaf of time;
Stubborn hopes are built
Around the gilded, brittle body-bubble.
But India taught me to love

– Paramahansa Yogananda,
from "My India"

In March of 2016, my wife, Sheridan, and I set out on an exploratory journey to India and Sri Lanka to gather information for a sequel to my first book, The Lhasa

Trilogy. As far as India is concerned, though, planned events are never as they seem to be, and the traveler must learn to expect the unexpected.

I had gone there once before in 1992 to seek out miracle workers, previously described in my book, Oklahoma Is Where I Live. As I suggested in that writing, spiritual saints were few and far between. Still, a miracle occurred not only in India, but also on my return home, when my rose-colored glasses were abruptly ripped from my face. The illusions I had previously swallowed, hook, line, and sinker, disintegrated into the ethers, revealing the stark, shocking truth about my life. While extremely painful at the time, this newfound wisdom eventually transported me into a far better existence, and I will be forever grateful to India for being the catalyst that set the wheels in motion. But that was then, and I couldn't help but wonder: What surprises await me this time?

Everything started innocently enough. After painstaking research and pondering carefully what I wanted to write about, we set our travel plans. First, we were to depart from Oklahoma City, eventually landing in New Delhi. From there, we would fly to Goa, where we would take a four-hour drive over the mountains to Hubli. Then we would motor to Mundgod and visit my longtime friend, Gen Tsesum Tashi, an eighty-eight-year-old Tibetan monk. Next, we would drive to the ancient Badami Cave Temples, followed by a flight to Agra to view the awe-inspiring Taj Mahal. Afterward, to Aurangabad, to walk through the mystical Ellora and Ajanta caves. Our last day in India would be in Mumbai, where we would fly to Sri Lanka for the final leg of our tour.

While I could write a tome about our varied experiences in India, one precious, sacred event stands out in my mind, and that was the time spent with Gen Tsesum Tashi. I began sponsoring him over twenty years ago when I attended a Tibetan fundraiser in Norman, Oklahoma, and picked his picture from a stack of photographs of monks who needed patrons. He was much older than the others, yet his gentle, kind features drew my attention to him. Since that time, I have supported him with a small, monthly donation that provided for some of his basic needs. We have continued as pen pals over those two decades, and he contributed a great deal of background information as I wrote The Lhasa Trilogy. While I was looking forward to seeing him, I must confess I was a bit anxious about our first in-person meeting and wondered how things would go.

After leaving from Hubli that fateful morning, our driver zigzagged on a confusing route through the middle of nowhere in rural India. Yet, his efforts were rewarded as we finally found the Gen Tsesum Tashi's residence in the Tibetan colony, situated just outside of Mundgod. As we entered his small, cozy quarters, the first thing that struck me was his smile, radiant with love, reminding me much of the Dalai Lama. After introducing ourselves, I asked him, through the assistance of a translator, to tell us the story of his travels from Tibet. He related that shortly after the Dalai Lama left Tibet, he exited his beloved country along with a small group of Tibetans. They traversed through the mountain passes into Bhutan, where they were attacked by Chinese bombers. After many travails during the arduous journey, they finally arrived at a refugee camp in northeast India. Eventually, they relocated to Mundgod in the southern part of the country, where he has lived ever since.

After presenting Gen Tsesum Tashi with some small gifts, I asked if Sheridan and I could meditate with him, and we agreed to sit for fifteen minutes. I closed my eyes, focused on my breath, and after a bit glanced down at my watch. The prescribed time had passed, but my monk friend was still deep in meditation, eyes closed, fingers rhythmically moving his prayer beads, his head slowly rocking back and forth. I went back into meditation, and fifteen more minutes passed, yet he remained immersed in his contemplation. Once again, I closed my eyes, and after a total of forty-five minutes, Gen Tsesum Tashi continued on, oblivious to the world. At that point, I glanced over at one of the other monks in attendance, who stood and walked over to gently arouse him.

When Gen Tsesum Tashi became conscious of his environment, once again there was that smile, that beaming, beautiful smile. A short time later, as Sheridan and I were preparing to leave, he said to me, "I know I am an old man, but I hope that before I die, I will see you again." I replied, "Of course, I'd like to see you as well." We smiled, clasped hands, and as we bowed to each other, we accidentally bumped heads, bringing a chuckle to us both. When Sheridan and I walked out of the door, tears formed in my eyes as I realized I was leaving the presence of an old, dear friend. I wondered: Will I ever see him again?

God only knows . . .

Now, as I look back, I realize that Gen Tsesum Tashi had spent much of his life devoted to his meditation practice. His technique had become so finely tuned that he was effortlessly able to go into samadhi, an experience of divine ecstasy where the human consciousness becomes one with cosmic consciousness. Samadhi is a state of mind all meditators aspire to; certainly I do, and to witness that ecstatic state firsthand was a blessing beyond measure. For me, meeting Gen

Tsesum Tashi was the unexpected and delightful surprise I had been waiting for on this trip. While the path of spiritual growth can often be painful, it doesn't have to be.

So, what is India? The best way I can describe it is a steamy, sweaty blend of poverty, spirituality, filth, beauty, and challenges. India can be a wondrous place of self-exploration, but it is certainly not for the faint of heart, nor those seeking a light, easy-going adventure. As I ponder India, a land of mystery and diversity, a kaleidoscope of images roll through my mind: cattle wandering through busy city streets, acting as if they own the place – women adorned with beautiful saris, no matter how destitute their conditions – copious, foul-smelling diarrhea – bright, loving, curious smiles – women slapping their laundry on rocks in polluted, murky green lakes – cell phones in nearly everyone's hands – sweltering, penetrating heat – men urinating by the roadside – the stunning beauty of the Taj Mahal – wild monkeys pilfering handbags from terrified tourists – snorting black pigs rooting through ubiquitous piles of rotting trash – pleading beggars holding their hands out – bathrooms without toilet paper or sinks – tasty, spicy food that is guaranteed to make steam come out of the ears – friendly, loving, peaceful people. India is an enigma beyond description, a milieu unlike anywhere else in the world. Yet, underlying all the sticky, odorous morass is an inherent, ancient spirituality, bathed in glowing love, just waiting to be discovered.

The next time I'm ready to be tested, reconfigured, and raised to the next level of spirituality, I'd like to return. Like Paramahansa Yogananda, I love India, with all of the intensity and growth opportunities she offers.

Besides, I've got a Tibetan friend I'd like to see again.

Chapter Ten

CHOPPING COTTON

My brother, Jim, and,
Trudging through a scorching field,
Up and down a planted row
Sharpened hoe in hand.
The sun bears down
Through a cloudless sky.
Sweating profusely,
No wind,
Only heat,
Dry as a bone,
Unbearable.
Yet we walk on.
Duty calls us.
We are protectors of puffs of snowy white,
Knights without armor,
Saints of the cotton field.

∞∞∞

Thanks to us,
No weeds are safe,
No matter how well they hide,
Like chameleons,
Almost invisible.
Yet we see them lurking,
We sense their terror,
And silent screams.
With a flash of steel
They are cut down,
Severed,
Lifeless,
Desiccating.

∞∞∞

Earlier that morning,
We were dropped off by our Dad
With lunches and a water jug
And a promise he would return that evening.
And he always did
Thank God.

∞∞∞

For a seeming eternity
We steadily walk, hacking, slicing, attacking.
The sun imperceptibly crosses the sky.
As the shadows deepen.
Our pace slows,
Lips parched,
Bodies aching,
And yet we walk on,

Until we see a trail of dust
Behind a familiar pickup.
Exhilaration!
Joy beyond imagining!
We collectively sigh,
Our pace quickens,
Though our feet drag in the dusty loam.
Soon we would be home.
Hot shower,
Clean clothes.
Home-cooked food,
Ice-cold water to drink,
Lots of it.
And yet we knew
That next morning we would rise from our beds
And return once more
To a place where vultures circle,
Death Valley.

∞∞∞

Now those times have passed
And as I look back
I realize such work builds character,
Inner strength,
Fortitude.
But . . .
While I have no doubt that is true,
I hope I never again find myself
Mired in misery.
Wondering if each step will be my last.
Chopping cotton

Chapter Eleven

GLOWWORMS

O Greater Light, we praise Thee for the less;
The eastern light our spires touch at morning,
The light that slants upon our western doors
at evening.
The twilight over stagnant pools at batflight,
Moon light and star light, owl and moth light,
Glowworm glowlight on a grassblade.
O Light Invisible, we worship Thee!
– T. S. Eliot, from *O Light Invisible*

We are all worms. But I believe that I am
a glowworm.
– Winston Churchill

When Sheridan and I were recently vacationing in
Santa Fe, we visited our friends, Larry and Barbie, and over
some good red wine and tasty edibles, Larry mentioned that

some time ago, he had the sublime experience of seeing a glowworm. I was stunned. *A glowworm?* The only thing I knew about glow worms was the uplifting, toe-tapping song sung by the Mills Brothers I had heard as a child:

Shine little glowworm, glimmer, glimmer
Shine little glowworm, glimmer, glimmer
Lead us lest too far we wander
Love's sweet voice is calling yonder
Shine little glowworm, glimmer, glimmer
Hey, there don't get dimmer, dimmer
Light the path below, above
And lead us on to love!

I hated to confess that I had never seen a glowworm, but Larry's rather offhand comment planted a seed thought in my mind and kindled a strong desire to gaze at one myself. After all, how many of us have been lucky enough to see a glowworm?

The next day Sheridan and I were having breakfast at a lovely Santa Fe B & B, Ravens Ridge, when I casually asked the proprietors, Judge and Phyllis, "Hey, have either of you ever seen a glowworm before?"

To my surprise, Judge said, "Why, yes, I saw one just a year or so ago."

My eyes widened, and I stammered, "Wh . . . Where?"

Pointing, he said, "I saw one crawling on the wall next to the garden area. It was quite beautiful."

I couldn't believe my good fortune; Santa Fe seemed to be in the middle of a veritable glowworm colony.

Later, Sheridan and I left to enjoy our day, but on that night and those that followed, I excused myself and disappeared into the verdant Ravens Ridge garden, a man on a mission, searching high and low for the object of my desire, a glowworm. Alas, in spite of my determined, persistent efforts, not a single one of the glimmering creatures made an appearance. The last night there, as I sat expectantly on a bench overlooking the garden, I finally realized that finding a glowworm was much like a spiritual experience, in that while one can set the stage for such a sacred event, one cannot force it to occur. Rather, such a hallowed moment usually comes of its own volition. I sighed and slowly walked back to our room, disappointed but hoping that somehow, someway, I would eventually find the elusive glowworm.

Returning home, I did some online research and discovered that in America, a glowworm could be not only the larval stage of the firefly, but also a railroad worm, a member of a bioluminescent beetle family. If you happen to live down under – in Australia or New Zealand – glowworms are not beetles, but instead flies called fungus gnats. One genus, *Arachnocampa*, lives on the ceilings of caves, where they light up the interior with a soft, almost fluorescent blue light that has all the appearance of a van Gogh-like starry night sky.

I wondered: *Why does the glowworm capture such interest?* Certainly, not many worms or insects have had songs written about them, "La Cucaracha" being a notable exception. One explanation must be the bioluminescence itself, which occurs not only in glowworms and fireflies, but also in some forms of marine life, certain fungi, and bacteria. While scientists can explain the biochemical basis for this phenomenon, for me, the soft, shining light conjures up mystical, magical, and ethereal feelings, thoughts of fairy dust, and the elemental kingdom. Also, for fireflies in particular,

I find myself moved by the innocence of such tiny insects, yet, amazingly enough, they wield the seemingly miraculous power to generate light. Perhaps even more significant, when I gaze at a firefly flitting through the dark night, the pulsing luminescence reminds me of the soul, the radiant spark of God that lies deep within each of us. I believe this divine part of our being remains pure and holy and cannot be sullied by our missteps. In that way, referring to the words of Winston Churchill, indeed we *all* are glowworms.

Despite the onerous challenge of my search, I plan to steadfastly continue my quest for the elusive glowworm. I expect that in the nights to come, I will be out methodically searching various environs into the wee hours. So, if you happen to hear someone rustling around in the bushes outside your home on a pitch-black, new moon night, don't be too concerned. It's likely just yours truly, searching for my little bioluminescent friend. When I find her, I will rejoice, and you are likely to hear a piercing scream of uninhibited joy.

Will my eventual discovery be a spiritual experience?
How could it be otherwise?

Chapter Twelve

As Above. So Below

Not long ago, I stretched out on a reclining chair in the back yard, resting and contemplating. I gazed up at the evening sun as it reddened and slowly sank behind the trees. Birds excitedly twittered their final messages and alerts before nightfall, and leaves rustled as a gentle breeze wafted through them. Nearby our dogs, Karma and Buddy, gnawed contentedly on their rawhide chews. In that idyllic moment, the realization occurred to me that the wind is much like my breath, the sun is as my heart, and the chatter of birds is akin to my thoughts. I intimately understood, as is said in Genesis, that God created us in His image, and what a blessing that is.

As above, so below.

Chapter Thirteen

A Moment In Time

Some afternoons, I like to take a dip in the pool, and then recline on a lawn chair and mindfully observe the happenings in the back yard. Surprisingly enough, a lot of action is taking place, if I simply have eyes to see.

Just the other day, the weather was warm and balmy, and the light breeze that brushed across my face brought to life the wind chimes hanging next to Sheridan's and my home, catching me by surprise with a lilting melody that emanated from the midst of silence. The sun was gradually falling behind the oak trees that flourish on our property, with a bright corona that contrasted with the dark green of the leaves and the royal blue of the sky. Our dogs, Karma and Buddy, were delighted that I was hanging around with them, and every so often, they presented themselves for petting, their bright, innocent eyes filling me with joy. After I rubbed their furry heads and told them what good dogs there were, they frolicked and played, taking turns chasing each other around the backyard and barking at the chattering squirrels that taunted them from the trees.

As the evening progressed and the sun sank lower in the sky, I could hear the light, oscillating sounds of cicadas and tree frogs arising from the woods to the south, accompanied by the comforting coos of mourning doves. When I gazed upward, I saw Mississippi kites circling slowly overhead, looking for prey, prepared to streak down through the darkening sky at a moment's notice. Looking straight ahead toward the hummingbird wind chime hanging from a tree branch over the pool, I became amused when I discovered a blue dragonfly clinging to the string of the chime. Over the past few weeks, I've noticed the same event repeatedly, and I found myself wondering what those beautiful insects were thinking. Did they believe that the plastic hummingbird was a giant dragonfly, protecting them from creatures that would do them harm? Was there some sort of romantic attraction? Was the string simply in a convenient place for a siesta? One can only guess, but I smiled as I thought of the possibilities.

My mind started to wander, and I began pondering the events of my life, some happy, some sad, though in that hallowed moment, any concerns I had dissolved into the ethers, and I was filled with contentment. I started to doze, and brief, mellow dreams moved in and out of my consciousness. I immersed myself in the restorative milieu of the backyard, letting the energy surround me. I knew that I was healing, inside and out, and I felt grateful. As the Zen Buddhist master Thich Nhat Hanh once said, "Present moment, wonderful moment."

I couldn't have said it better myself.

Chapter Fourteen

When I Am Gone

When I am gone
    Screeching hawks will still circle the sky,
    Open-mouthed baby birds will cry for food,
    The sun will circle the heavens,
    The moon will softly glow in the night.
When I am gone
    Fireflies will still make us dream of fairies,
    Rains will nourish the sweltering Earth,
    Fragrant wisteria blooms will bless and heal us,
    Sparkling rainbows will remind us of God.
When I am gone
    Crystalline streams will still rush through the
    mountains,
    Falling stars will make us catch our breath,
    Verdant forests will demand our silence,
    The ocean will beckon us to walk alongside her.
When I am gone,
    Or am I ever?

Even though my body no longer walks the Earth,
My soul continues on its journey,
Wherever that may be.
I will always recall the love we shared,
Little kindnesses you freely gave,
Precious moments,
Soft smiles,
Gentle touches.
I am never gone
And neither are you,
And neither is anyone.
We are eternal,
Infinite sparks in the body of God.
Yes, love is always remembered,
No matter what form our souls take,
As it does for all who unconditionally care.
Whatever the relationship,
Love will inextricably bind us
For eternity.

Chapter Fifteen

The Son I Never Knew

Sometimes, I wonder
What my son would look like now
If he had survived
The devastating tragedy of February 12, 1979
The day of his childbirth,
The day he died.
Sometimes, flashes cross my mind from
that fateful time,
Moments magnified, agonizing, gut-wrenching,
Ones that take my breath away.
Yet, in the midst of the chaos,
I see his newborn face.
He is so beautiful.
Sometimes, I miss the moments we
should have had together,
Changing his diapers,
Watching him take his first steps,
Wiping his tears,

Seeing him off to school,
Little joys, never shared.
Time heals all wounds – or so they say . . .
Yet, year after year, on Memorial Day,
I tearfully stand before his lonely grave,
And gaze down at the cold, rose granite marker.
I look at his name etched upon it,
Aware that dusty, cremated remains lie below,
Remnants of a baby that once lived and breathed
My baby . . .
I feel an odd mixture of sadness, anger,
and remorse,
And I wonder what might have been.
I breathe deeply, in and out, and I try
to understand,
And yet . . . I never do.

Chapter Sixteen

SMARTPHONES, TOOLS OR TRAPS?

"The most precious gift we can offer others is our presence. When mindfulness embraces those we love, they will bloom like flowers."

– Thich Nhat Hanh

Distractions that stop us from giving our full attention to others have existed since time immemorial. In the prehistoric era, I can picture a cavewoman having an engaging conversation with her caveman husband. She complains about how cold the cave was last night, and how she wishes she had more furs to keep warm. He describes how hard his day was, with no success on the hunt, and how hungry he feels. The discussion was going well until he became entranced by the sight of a saber-tooth tiger fighting with a woolly mammoth outside their cave. Frustrated by his sudden lack of attentiveness, she boots him out of the cave, only to discover the next morning that the saber-tooth tiger had decided her husband was easier to take down and was a much tastier meal than the woolly mammoth.

Or imagine in ancient Egypt, Mark Antony and Cleopatra are in their well-appointed palace, eating a sumptuous snack of figs and grapes. He wants to chat with her about their problem-child daughter, Cleopatra Selene, who had been flirting with the next-door neighbor's son. While Mark is tearfully baring his heart and soul, he abruptly realizes that Cleopatra is staring through the open window at an attractive, muscular slave boy working in the garden. Angry and seriously thinking about strangling his Egyptian lover, he yells "Stercore!" – Latin for "Shit!"— throws his heavy golden goblet of wine against the wall and stalks out of the room.

In more recent times, while not nearly as dramatic as the historical scenes described above, the television has captivated many a man who preferred to watch a football game on his big-screen TV rather than listen to the demands of his wife or children.

The latest in our longstanding history of compelling distractions is not the saber-tooth tiger, the woolly mammoth, the sensuous slave boy, or a football game; rather, it's the smartphone. Some version of this device seems to be in everyone's hand. For example, when I was in India last year, even among the poorest of the poor, many were chit-chatting on mobile phones nonstop. *Why is that?* one might ask. My theory is that never has such an intoxicating and powerful technological instrument been so readily available to John Q. Public.

In the not-so-distant past, access to the wisdom of the universe was limited to astrophysicists, nuclear scientists, and highbrow, ivory- tower intellectuals, who were willing to spend long hours digging through dusty tomes in the hidden recesses of a library. Now, anyone with a smartphone can search through the world's vast storehouse of information at a moment's notice. For example: What makes a Tasmanian devil so devilish? Look it up! What was Beethoven's favorite food? Look it up! (It was macaroni with butter and cheese, by the way).

Besides the Internet, another fringe benefit of the smartphone is that a person can communicate with anyone, anytime. Need to say "hi" to a friend? Knock out a text. Want to wish a happy birthday to a sister who lives in Albania? Make a quick call. Without limits or boundaries. the world lies at one's fingertips. Also, with a smartphone, the public has the rather amazing capability to keep in touch with all the latest happenings. To make sure you miss out on nothing and receive information instantaneously, a notification beep goes off whenever an email, tweet, or news flash is received.

And what about gaming and apps? When someone is between appointments, what better way to kill time than to enjoy an entertaining game of Solitaire or perhaps snoop around the local environs in search of a rare Pokemon? Or, depending on one's mood and inclination, maybe download some new apps and explore other games or programs?

One problem with this immediacy of information, communication, and entertainment is its incredible allure. When I hear that mesmerizing beep, it draws me to my smartphone much like a mythological Greek siren, and it takes all the willpower I can muster to resist its seductive call. Most of us will drop whatever we are doing to discover the meaning of that captivating signal. What could the beep represent? *Did the Oklahoma City Thunder win their last basketball game? Did a tornado alert get issued for my area? Did I win the lottery?*

What is the solution to this all-consuming madness? I believe Zen Master Thich Nhat Hanh would patiently inform us that the answer lies in mindfulness, and one should give full attention to whatever is happening in the present moment. While certainly there are times when multitasking is important, in most instances it's best to keep the mind one-pointed. To give a few examples: *Driving a car?* Try to ignore the beep from the smartphone, especially if motoring on the interstate going seventy miles-per-hour in bumper-to-bumper traffic. Even a quick glance to discover the source of the beep could be risky business. *Having lunch with friends?* Unless one needs to be available for life-or-death emergencies, leave the smartphone in the car. Close companions deserve one's complete attention and nothing less. *Taking a stroll outside?* Try putting the smartphone on silent, slip it into a pocket and quietly, introspectively, observe the surroundings. One might hear a bird singing a lilting melody, see an ant scurrying by on the grass, enjoy a nod and wave from a stranger, and, one can only hope, view an orange and black monarch butterfly majestically soaring into a deep-blue, cloudless sky. One might be surprised at the beauty and interconnections that can be discovered, if one is only willing to observe them.

In my way of thinking, the goal should be to own our smartphones, but not be owned by them. While technology is an essential aspect of our society and is to be valued, far more meaningful is our connectedness to humanity and nature. If Buddha walked among us, he would recommend the Middle Path, not being extreme in any one direction. As I ponder his wisdom, I realize that could also include the appropriate, measured use of smartphones.

So, if you *had* to pick one over the other, would you choose to notice the smile of a passerby or keep up with the latest minutia of the news?

For me, it's an easy call ... I mean choice.

Chapter Seventeen

His Eye Is On The Sparrow

As a boy, something powerful took place when I was armed with my BB gun. When the weapon was loaded and tightly clutched in my arms, nothing frightened me. No wild animal, no matter how fierce or ferocious, had a chance against me and my killing machine. I smile now as I realize that reality and illusion are sometimes hard to separate, and this goes not only for children, but also for adults.

My favorite place to exercise my dominance over all living things existed in the countryside around my grandparents' modest home near the rural town of Friendship, Oklahoma. My brother Jim and I would prowl about our private hunting ground in pursuit of quarry, firing off our guns at anything that moved, hoping to demonstrate our machismo to the world around us. As described in *Oklahoma Is Where I Live,* we rarely actually shot anything, but one day I did, and that became a moment I will never forget.

∞∞∞

One warm, toasty summer day, Jim and I, along with my sister, Connie, were blessed to spend a week in Friendship with our grandparents, affectionately called Papa and Mama. I always thought that the reason for such vacations was to give our grandparents some quality time with us while school was out for the summer. Somehow it never occurred to me that Mom and Dad might have needed some quiet moments together without having to handle their three rambunctious kids. Of all of us, Connie was the least likely to be difficult, while my brother and I were constantly taunting each other, and I suspect that might be at least part of the reason for my father's early hair loss.

Leaving our sister behind under my grandmother's protective watch, Jim and I set out looking for something to kill. At first, we focused on shooting inanimate objects such as tin cans or glass jars in the trash heap northeast of the barn. Soon we were satisfied that our aims were so good we could have given sharpshooting lessons to Wyatt Earp. We returned to the outbuildings around the house, quietly skulking around, keeping our eyes peeled for anything that moved.

Disappointed that no savage, snarling wild animals were to be found, we began to focus on smaller game, such as the birds that frequented the area. Starlings, house sparrows, robins, and such, were all fair game. Shot after shot went off, but the twittering birds didn't seem to notice as the BBs buzzed all around them. Just as I was about to run out of ammunition, the unexpected happened; I actually hit a bird, and it fell from the telephone line where moments before, it had been happily singing its songs.

Shocked, Jim and I ran over to the place where it landed. The bird, with black and white wings and a silver-grey head and chest, was lifeless – not gasping for breath, not even a twitch. The spot on the bird where the BB had struck was not visible. The bird was beautiful, but it was dead. I felt an odd mixture of pride and shame. Because my shot had been true, but the bird would never twitter its song again.

Thinking that my grandmother could identify the bird and perhaps offer me some words of comfort, I rushed through the back door of the home and yelled, "Mama! I've shot a bird. Come see!"

From another part of the house, I heard her say, "I'll be right there after I get Connie settled down."

I waited by the door until she appeared, her warm smiling face beaming love to me. "Where is it?"

"Follow me," I said.

In a few moments, we arrived, Jim still standing by the dead bird. Mama kneeled down beside it and stared at its lifeless body.

"Oh my," she said with a twinge of sadness in her voice, "it's a mockingbird. I love how they sing in the morning."

Hearing her words, I felt my face redden with guilt. *She'll no longer hear this bird's song*, I thought.

Seeing my reaction, she said in a soothing way, "It's okay, Gary. Don't worry about it. There are plenty of birds to go around." With that, she patted me on the shoulder and walked back to the home to continue taking care of Connie and her household chores, leaving Jim and me alone with the bird that I had shot in cold blood.

What to do?

Remorseful, sad, and ridden with shame, I said to Jim, "We need to bury it."

Jim nodded his approval, and with our hands, we dug

through the loose, sandy soil, creating a nice-sized hole. We then found two small sticks and bound them together in the shape of a cross with strands of dead grass.

After planting the cross at the head of our makeshift grave, I placed the little bird in the hole and covered it with soil.

Task completed, Jim and I stood gazing at the tiny gravesite for a bit, though we both knew that for a proper burial, someone had to pray. We closed our eyes and bowed our heads. I briefly said, "Dear God, bless this little bird. I'm sorry that I shot it. Amen."

With that, we slowly walked away, and I tearfully promised myself that I would never lift a gun again to shoot at an animal of any kind.

And I haven't.

∞∞∞

Now, many years later, as I think back on this incident, it still brings tears to my eyes, and I am reminded of the words from the old church song, *His Eye Is on the Sparrow*:

> *Why should I feel discouraged?*
> *Why should the shadows come?*
> *Why should my heart be lonely?*
> *And long for heav'n and home.*
> *When Jesus is my portion?*
> *My constant friend is he.*
> *His eye is on the sparrow,*
> *And I know he watches me.*
> *His eye is on the sparrow,*
> *And I know he watches me.*

With the benefit of time, experience, and perhaps a bit more wisdom, I believe that all of creation, whether mineral, plant, animal, or human, are inexorably linked in consciousness. This consciousness, what some would call God, is aware of all things, even the sparrow, or in the situation of my youth, the mockingbird. When that little bird was shot from the telephone line, I feel certain that God knew of it. Now, many years later, as I read Matthew, 6:26, I find some modicum of comfort.

Look at the birds of the air; they neither sow nor reap nor gather into barns, and yet your heavenly Father feeds them. Are you not of more value than they?
Amen.

Chapter Eighteen

Wind Chimes

I love wind chimes. Something about the random, unpredictable rhythm of gentle peals affects me in a positive, uplifting way. Also, I am quite fond of the oscillating resonance of a Tibetan singing bowl. As I chime it by rubbing a mallet around the upper rim in a circular motion, pure, clear sounds emanate from the bowl. The varied, fluctuating tones are mystical, centering, and have a soothing effect, much like the soft crooning of a mother to her newborn infant.

When I think of absorbing settings, no doubt the master producer is nature itself, far superior to Cecil B. De-Mille's mammoth undertakings. The distinctive hum of cicadas as nighttime begins to approach, tree frogs croaking their rhythmic tunes, birds twittering their melodies, along with the gurgling of moving water and the peaceful rustling of wind blowing through the trees – all are balms to my soul. The sounds of nature are much like an orchestra, each contributing unique musical notes to the symphony. Put all together, they beat "The Ten Commandments" by a long shot, with Chuck Heston and his wild, flowing Moses hair leading the nation of Israel through the parting Red Sea.

Speaking of music, I continue to be amazed at how it affects me. For example, when I hear a string quartet playing Haydn, I find myself completely engrossed by the melody. During some movements, especially the Largo of Opus 76, No. 5, I often well up with tears as I sense the deep emotion Haydn so aptly portrays. When I hear the Finale of that same quartet, I find myself giggling like a little boy, amazed at the spontaneity and joy leaping from the creative genius of Haydn into my heart and head.

Some music has a completely opposite effect on me. The repetitive drone of rap – with its sometimes violent, disturbing lyrics – tends to make me irritable. Not that I listen to it intentionally, but sometimes, say in a store, it's played in the background. At some point, I become aware of an agitation in myself and realize the cause for my unsettled feeling. I sigh and either leave the area or consciously shield the noise from my mind. If the latter fails, a speedy exit is often the only solution.

Life, with its up and downs, often requires a retreat at the end of the day to heal from the intentional or unintentional wounds inflicted upon us. With my sometimes overpowering, frenzied work in emergency medicine, such a refuge is an absolute necessity.

My healing sanctuary awaits in the backyard. There, I can sit back and relax, listen to the wind chimes toning gently in the background, watch the evening sun peeking through the trees, lightly kissing me with his warm, calming touch, and see the unconditional love in my dogs' eyes as I pet their soft, furry heads. Usually, after a few, slow deep, centering breaths, I find balance and peace of mind returning once again.

Taking care of yourself and your needs is not selfish; rather, it's a necessary part of allowing you to do your soul's work, whatever that might be. In the meantime, I'm thinking of obtaining another set of wind chimes to put in my back-yard. Trust me, with the stressful work I do, I need all the help I can get.

Don't we all?

Chapter Nineteen

TEXTING

While you were texting,
You never saw the smile on your loved one's face,
The twinkle in her eyes,
Her arms as she reached out to you,
Or heard her caring words.
While you were texting,
Precious moments passed by,
Ones that could have been shared with others,
Ones that could have been filled with meaning.
Instead, you chose to focus your attention on a device,
Picking out letters on a sterile, unfeeling keyboard,
Ignoring the world around you,
A world that begs you to embrace it,
In all its beauty and complexity.
The glories of technology
Can never replace the sparkle of a dewdrop,
The luminous corona of the sun,
The hummingbird as it darts about,

The juicy taste of a ripened peach,
Or the smell of freshly-turned earth.
An opposite exists to mindfulness,
And that is
Texting.

Chapter Twenty

FEAR

Being a senior medical student is living the good life. Most of the required rotations, such as surgery – the epitome of pain and suffering – internal medicine, OB/GYN, and pediatrics, have been completed in the third year, so in the fourth, the senior student is free to select experiences that provide learning and enjoyment. Usually, these are rotations that place little or no constraints on one's time, as at this point in medical training, the student has suffered enough sleepless, bleary-eyed moments on call and seventy-plus-hour work weeks.

Yes, things couldn't be better, and during these Life of Riley times, I chose to fulfill a longstanding desire to get my pilot's license. So, over the course of the final six months of my senior year in medical school, I made regular trips to Max Westheimer Airport in Norman, Oklahoma, to take flying lessons. At least once a week, I boarded a rented Cessna 150 with my instructor and took to the skies. Before long, I had mastered takeoffs, landings, and how to recover from stalls. I performed touch and go landings at a number of rural airports to be certain I was comfortable flying to other places where I had never been. After I satisfied my solo requirements and passed a written exam, I took to the air to be tested by the FAA, and I was certified as a private pilot. No longer was I constrained to the ground. I was literally and figuratively as free as a bird. Hallelujah!

∞∞∞

As I've noted in previous writings, the residency program I entered after medical school was extremely challenging. Given the limitations on time, it was a near miracle that I could find any free moments to fly, even though I was chomping at the bit to do so. The location of my residency was in southern California, and after a bit of searching, I found a local airport, Riverside Municipal, that I could use as a base of operations. Once I presented my licensure paperwork and was checked out on a test flight by a local rental company, I was approved to take out airplanes for some jaunts into the big blue sky.

I experienced a handful of airborne adventures before I had the brilliant idea to invite Adam, one of my senior residents, to come along on an afternoon flight. *What better way to make a good impression?*, I thought, unaware of the predicament we were about to get into.

When we lifted off that day, the sky was clear blue and cloudless. I confidently flew over the beautiful snow-capped San Bernardino Mountains, taking in the blues of Lake Arrowhead and Big Bear Lake, which starkly contrasted with the surrounding arid desert landscape moving underneath us.

I felt moved by the view and said, "God, Adam, is that beautiful or what?"

He brushed back his dark, straight hair with his right hand and continued to gaze at the landscape through his thick, black-frame glasses. "I couldn't agree more."

The area was too gorgeous for words, and after leisurely circling for a while, I glanced at my watch and knew it was time to return. As I turned the airplane and headed back towards the airport, I discovered to my great consternation, that it was buried underneath a thick layer of suffocating smog and was nowhere to be seen.

I felt a surge of panic, though I tried my best not to demonstrate my anxieties to Adam. I was VFR (Visual Flight Rules) certified, but not IFR (Instrument Flight Rules). In other words, I was qualified to fly in fair weather only, relying on visual landmarks, such as bodies of water, mountains, and highways, and I had to be on the watch to avoid other aircraft. *But now*, I thought, *where was the airport?*

Fortunately, Riverside had a nearby VORTAC (VHF Omnidirectional Range/Tactical Aircraft Control), which allowed me to know the airport's geographical location, even though I could not see it. I headed toward the airport, and soon enough, I crossed over it.

Arriving there, I could see several other airplanes circling above the smog. I decided to radio the control tower to get some much-needed help.

I said, "Control tower?"

"Affirmative."

"This is November One Fife Tree Niner Niner."

"Roger that."

"I am circling above the airport, and I am VFR rated, not IFR. What am I to do?"

I noticed that Adam was starting to look a bit nervous. His already light complexion started to whiten even more. If this kept up, he would look more like Casper the Friendly Ghost than a human being.

"Roger that. The smog is so dense we have placed the airport in Special VFR."

I had never heard this term before. "What does that mean?"

Adam had now developed a thin sheen of sweat on his forehead. I could almost hear him thinking, *What do you mean you don't know? What in the hell am I doing here?*

"Roger that. Since the weather conditions are not suitable for VFR pilots, I'll call your number when it is your turn to land." Repeating, you are November One Fife Tree Niner Niner, right?"

"Affirmative. Wilco."

We circled above the smog for a while, and then I began to wonder, *Should I go a little lower and see if I can visualize the runway? Maybe get a better feel for the situation?*

Adam began to squirm as I dipped down into the smoggy soup. Still unable to see anything clearly, I went a little lower. It was then that I heard the buzz of another airplane, and I stifled a scream and sharply veered to the left as the plane flew directly across my path. I had barely avoided a midair collision.

I looked over at Adam. He was trembling and deathly silent. I suspected that he was even more nervous than I was. At least I had some control over the situation, while he had none. I felt badly that I had put him through this.

Somehow the control tower saw what had occurred through the dense smog. "November One Fife Tree Niner Niner?"

"Roger," I blurted out, my heart still in my throat.

"Come down now. You are cleared to land. Please stop by the control tower once you have secured your airplane."

Once I'd landed and parked the plane, I left Adam in the car to gather his wits about him. I walked into the control tower, and a friendly man with a long-sleeved white shirt and blue-patterned narrow tie greeted me. He looked me in the eye and said, "Do you understand Special VFR?"

"I thought I did."

"Just to be clear, the next time you fly in these conditions, please stay above the smog until your number is called. That way, we can avoid any future mishaps. Where are you from?"

"Oklahoma."

"I might guess that you've never had to deal with situations like this before."

"Roger that."

"Well, now you've learned, and you're no worse off. Be careful next time, okay?"

"I will be."

Walking away, I knew I would have to calm down my resident's nerves, and I also was aware that I would never pilot an airplane again.

And I haven't.

∞∞∞

After that episode, I have developed a somewhat moderate case of acrophobia, which has persisted to this day. That said, I have no problem getting into a plane, as long as I'm not flying it, and going up on elevators is easy. I do, however, get a bit edgy standing next to the railing of a balcony. While in the out-of-doors, I have strictly avoided rock climbing, and I'm not especially fond of exposed areas while hiking, especially where a misstep could cause a long fall down. In other words, my acrophobia could be a lot worse.

Many years later, I was hiking in Zion National Park with my friend Kevin. Since it had been quite some time since my near-death experience in California, I decided to challenge my fears and take on the famous Angels Landing trail, a hike known for its particularly exposed and narrow section leading up to the hair-raising viewpoint. The trek began at the Grotto Trailhead, and the hike up to the beginning of the *Oh-my-God* place was challenging, but only aerobically. When we approached the exposed portion, I knew it would be quite a gut check for me. The trail leads onto a narrow rock fin with a chain in the middle supported by metal posts embedded in the rock. Slip here, and it's a fifteen-hundred-foot drop off either side. I could just picture myself losing my balance and slipping off the edge, screaming at the top of my lungs as I plummeted to the rocky bottom, turning from Gary Conrad into an unrecognizable bloody pile of bones and flesh. I gaped open-mouthed as Kevin went ahead of me and practically danced over the exposed area. He actually seemed to be enjoying it.

On the other hand, I was completely petrified, and I clung to the chain as tightly as a drowning victim holds onto a life jacket. After walking just a hundred feet or so, I glanced down at my hands, and they were bleeding from being clenched so tautly on the chain. I decided then and there that this trek just wasn't worth it, and I slowly backtracked, inching my way along the fin back to safety.

What a relief it was to return to a place of security.

∞∞∞

Even now, as I think about my experience flying the airplane and the hike on Angels Landing, I get a tingle up and down my spine. While I believe it's admirable for intrepid souls to overcome their fears, some are just too challenging and buried too deep into the psyche. For me, it's enough that I recognize the source of my trepidation about heights, and I no longer have a burning desire to overcome it.

I'm only human, and that's okay.

Chapter Twenty-One

AN OCEAN OF WILDFLOWERS

After sixty-four years of life, one might guess that I would know when I needed to go to the wilderness to experience her healing caress. But older is not necessarily wiser . . .

The turmoil started around two weeks earlier, when I noticed that I was getting grumpy and argumentative. Besides that, events that would not normally bother me became blown out of proportion and assumed an exaggerated sense of importance. As my fuse became shorter, the pressure inside me ratcheted up, and I felt like a time bomb waiting to explode. Granted, I had recently been working more emergency department shifts than usual, and the cases that confronted me had been extremely challenging. Life and death decisions are never easy, and when I came home on such days, I was tired, irritable, and depleted.

After waiting far too long, I finally realized I was at the end of my rope and decided I needed to get away to the wilderness. Knowing I had the day free, I packed my trusty backpack, hopped into my white 2004 Honda CR-V, and headed for the Wichita Mountain Wildlife Refuge. This preserve in southwest Oklahoma was established in 1901 to protect wildlife at risk for extinction and to reintroduce species previously eliminated from the area. This included American bison, Rocky Mountain elk, Texas Longhorn cattle, wild turkeys, prairie dogs, river otters, and burrowing owls Have you ever seen a burrowing owl? I haven't, but I'd love to discover one someday.

Also a hiking Mecca, the preserve still oozes with the energy of the Native American peoples who once inhabited the area. I made the hour and a half drive in silence and focused on the road, while letting my consciousness randomly move in whatever direction it needed. I breathed deep, in and out, saying a silent prayer that I might find peace and healing at my destination, one of the most ancient mountain ranges in the Americas.

As I drove into the refuge, I was delighted to discover that recent rainfalls had caused the usually dry mountains and surrounding prairie lands to spring to life, and they were green, verdant, and full of expectant energy. After parking, I trekked through the rocky entrance of the Charon's Garden Wilderness and began to time my breathing with my steady, measured steps. Before long, I added my favorite mantra, given by Zen Buddhist monk Thich Nhat Hanh, repeating silently with my in and out breaths, *calming, smiling, present moment, wonderful moment.* Farther down the trail, I stopped my internal chanting and began softly singing "My Sweet Lord," by George Harrison, and later I switched to the old Christian classic, "Nearer, My God to Thee." I felt my consciousness expanding, and as I topped the plateau, I was finally able to catch sight of Crab Eyes, a pair of enormous round boulders perched on the crest of a rocky granite dome that seemed to peer across the plateau like a landlocked crustacean.

There, I was blessed by the grandeur of an ocean of beautiful wildflowers splayed out across the landscape. I caught my breath as blossoms of many varied colors, primarily yellows and reds, smiled at me. It seemed to me they were saying: *Troubled? Weary? Stay here and linger with us, and you will find comfort.* As I gazed at their magnificence, I was reminded of the words of Jesus, "Consider the lilies of the field, how they grow; they toil not, neither do they spin: yet I say unto you, that even Solomon in all his glory was not arrayed like one of these."

Indeed . . .

I walked across the grassy plateau, and after hiking a bit longer, chose a rocky outcrop hidden away from the trail, a place where I had a panoramic view of Crab Eyes. I fondly looked up at the unique formation, and, in my way of thinking, they represented the caring, comforting eyes of God, always aware of me and what I was going through, whatever the situation. I felt reassured and closed my eyes.

Once again, I focused on my breath, and I quietly listened inside and let the soothing peace of the wilderness flow into me. With time, I roused from my meditation, feeling refreshed and released from a good part of the heaviness that had previously pressed down on me. With Crab Eyes benevolently looking down at me, I opened my backpack and enjoyed a wilderness meal of a mandarin orange, native Oklahoma pecans, chocolate, and a granola bar. Once again, all felt right with the world. I sighed in contentment.

Lunch finished, I stood, shouldered my backpack and began trekking back down the faint path toward the trailhead. Once again, I experienced the beaming, joyful faces of the delicate, colorful wildflowers, and I wondered why I had waited so long to experience the healing effects of the wilderness. As I considered that thought, I realized that a healthy diet, exercise, and a regular meditation practice are simply not enough to sustain me through the trials and tribulations of working in the emergency department. Every so often, no matter how sound my physical, emotional, mental and spiritual practices might seem at the time, I still needed the benevolent nurturing of Mother Nature.

Next time, I promise that I will seek out the restorative powers of the wilderness before the situation gets out of hand. And maybe, just maybe, my wildflower friends will again be there to greet me.

Chapter Twenty-Two

AGING

"Old age comes on suddenly, and not gradually as is thought."

– Emily Dickinson

*W*here did the time go? Only yesterday, it seems, I was a young lad, fishing for crawdads, playing with our family dogs, Snappy and Mandy, scuffling with my brother Jim, incessantly pestering my little sister Connie, eating as much candy as I could get my hands on, and living the good life. My only responsibilities were taking a daily bath, brushing my teeth, performing my chores, going to school, and keeping in my parents' good graces. Those were happy times, the proverbial days of wine and roses, and the furthest thing from my mind was growing old.

Then came junior high and high school, with their associated adolescent crises and difficulties, college at Oklahoma State University, medical school, marriage, working in the emergency department, raising three lovely daughters, divorce, and eventually marriage to my true love, Sheridan. At that point, the writing bug bit me, and I feverishly authored five books over twelve years.

One recent, frosty winter morning, though, as I looked at myself in the bathroom mirror, I saw the beginning of jowls, a bald, shiny head, a sprinkling of white hairs in various, odd locations, and more wrinkles than I remembered, lots more. To my dismay, I suddenly realized *that person in the mirror is me, and he's sixty-eight years old.*

In disbelief, my first impulse was to look away, but then I courageously glanced again at this strange, aged man who was intently staring at me and perfectly matching my every move. Seemingly overnight, I had morphed from a sprightly, pink-cheeked, innocent youth into a moldering senior citizen.

As much as I hate to admit it, the unalterable truth is that now I am on Medicare and a lifetime, no-way-out member of the Geritol Generation. How could any right-minded person describe these times of inexorable decline as the "Golden Years?" If I had to take a guess, I might suppose that some out-of-work psychologist thought up this crazy notion while in a drug-induced stupor, just to make us feel better about our situation when we age.

So, now that I'm approaching the sunset of my life with the clouds becoming darker red and more menacing each day, what am I to do? *Is the Withering Heights Nursing Home and miserable decrepitude my only possible destiny? Should I accept my fate as immutable?*

As I asked these questions of myself, I thought back to my colleague and friend, Dr. Andrew Weil, who once said that the overall goal of aging was not to stop or reverse the natural aging process, aspirations that were simply not attainable, but rather, to achieve what some have called "compression of morbidity." In other words, by following a healthy lifestyle, the elderly can have a long and vigorous life, yet when death approaches, a rapid decline occurs, which most would agree is far better than lingering in painful misery. So, in expectation of achieving "compression of morbidity," as an integrative physician, here are my recommendations about how those ensconced in their senior years can still live well.

1. Stay active.
   Those who become sedentary have a tendency to stay that way.
2. Watch television in moderation.
   I used to drive for Mobile Meals and delivered food to the aged and infirm. I was astounded at how many were watching TV when I knocked on their front door. Too much television is mind-numbing and not conducive to a healthy brain.
3. Eat well.
   Diets rich in fresh fruits and vegetables are important and should be combined with a rich source of omega-3 fatty acids, such as wild-caught salmon. Enjoy whole grain products, avoid fried foods, and limit the intake of refined sugar, red meat, and white flour. By all means, though, at least occasionally live on the wild side and enjoy a rich, totally unhealthy meal. More importantly, don't feel guilty about it.
4. Maintain social connections.

To love and be loved is meaningful at any age, but this is especially true in the older population. Regularly call or meet with friends and family, and sometimes try to make new friends.

5. Always have something to look forward to.
    Activities such as travel, trying a new restaurant, or even attending the weekly bingo game are worth considering.

6. Keep your mind active.
    Crossword puzzles, sudoku, and any hobby you enjoy are avenues to keep the mind sharp. As the old saying goes, "If you don't use it, you lose it."

7. Avoid polypharmacy.
    You'd be amazed at the cornucopia of medications that well-intended physicians prescribe for elderly patients. Remember, every medicine has side effects and drug interactions of some kind. Multiply that by a long list of different prescriptions, and you've got a potential disaster on your hands.

8. Consider volunteer work.
    It's essential to believe that one still has a purpose in life.

As I have pondered the aging process, the more I have come to realize that with a bit of time, effort and persistence, the "Golden Years" can be just that. Granted, aging has its issues, but what about the positives? One usually has more free time to do what one wants, rather than being constrained by parenting children, a busy work schedule, or limited vacation time. More moments are available to spend with loved ones, and retirement can be a time of mellowness and reflection, a chance to learn, grow, and heal from the wounds of earlier years. Besides all that, growing old is an opportunity to deepen one's relationship with God, whether through spiritual texts, meditation, service to others, or wherever your soul leads you.

Someday, as much as I'd like to believe otherwise, I will die. Granted, at least part of what takes place before then is beyond my control, but I plan to follow my own advice and do all that I can to have a lifestyle that limits my eventual suffering and disability. After all, I've got a number of destinations yet to explore and many more books to write.

Something to look forward to?

Always.

Chapter Twenty-Three

ROADKILL

Early in the morning
When I drive to work,
I humbly pray to God
To help me through the day.
Every so often
In the midst of my prayers,
I discover a dead animal lying on the highway.
No, not just dead, but
Often mutilated and crushed,
Disfigured beyond recognition,
A disarrayed amalgam of blood, shattered
bones, and hair.
What was it?
A raccoon, a possum, a coyote, a skunk?
As I slow my car down,
I wonder what the circumstances were.
Perhaps the little creature was searching for food
Or looking for a mate?

Out for a midnight sashay?
As he sniffed around the road,
He somehow did not see
The lights bearing down on him,
A mechanical monster with glowing eyes,
Technology beyond his understanding,
Moving faster than he.
There was no escape.
After honking a warning
The rolling metal smashed into him,
Killing him instantly,
At least, I hope it did.
And so I pause briefly,
And I pray
For the little creature,
Asking God to bless his innocent soul.
Somehow, someway, I hope the animal knows,
That someone remembered his precious life,
If only for a moment

Chapter Twenty-Four

AUTUMN

"Autumn... the year's last, loveliest smile."
                                    – William Cullen Bryant

When I was a young lad, my favorite time of year was autumn. As I search back in my memories, several reasons come to mind. First, the sweltering days of summer had finally passed and were at long last behind me. While a certain joy came with never being cold, Oklahoma summers were nearly always miserable, blistering hot days, ones where your clothes became soaked with sweat at the slightest exertion. Yes, it was that bad. Autumn was the dessert, the reward for surviving the white-hot inferno of summer.

Even more importantly, the cooler days of fall brought with them every child's favorite holiday, Halloween, with the associated indescribable ecstasy of trick or treating. Being born with an insatiable sweet tooth, I would anxiously prepare for weeks for this grand occasion, the highlight of the year, a time when parental concerns about overdosing their children on unlimited amounts of sugar, artificial colors, and flavors were temporarily brushed aside.

To my young mind, the burning question was: *How can I go to as many houses as possible?* I planned my route with the precision of an Army general, relying on the previous year's experience to bypass the stingy places and zero in on the generous ones. I reasoned that the more homes I visited, the more candy I would get.

The most pressing concern that my brother, Jim, and I had was to convince our parents to chaperone our little sister, Connie. If we had to wait for her as she strolled along, casually hobnobbing with her friends who happened to cross our paths, our progress, and thus our haul, would have been significantly impeded. I loved my sis, but Halloween was serious business, and it was critical to pull out all the stops and eliminate unnecessary distractions. I would say to my parents something like this, "Hey, Mom and Dad, how about taking Connie with you for Halloween? Jim and I might go too fast for her, and we'd hate to accidentally leave her behind."

With these words, my parents' eyes widened, and they began to get nervous looks on their faces. Seeing my comments were having the desired effect, I added, "You know, it might not be safe. There are some strange people out there." When the words "safe" and "strange people" were invoked, all doubt was instantly erased from my parents' minds, and invariably my brother and I were allowed to go out on our own.

When the exalted, holy day of Halloween finally arrived, I would wear my best, pavement-gripping tennis shoes, so that I could sprint from home to home as quickly as my little legs could carry me. For the entire time, I was in a state of near panic, knowing I had only one shot at it for the year, and any planning mistakes I made would have to wait until next Halloween to correct. One especially annoying trap I occasionally fell into was when certain neighbors made the unfortunate decision to give healthy snacks for Halloween.

How dare they? Kids didn't go trick or treating to get apples, oranges, bananas, or other such nourishing treats. Especially hated were those little red boxes of Sun-Maid Raisins. *Yuck!* We only wanted the good stuff, candy that we could get sugar highs on, sweets that would mercilessly extract fillings for which our parents had paid their life savings. Health and Halloween simply didn't go together, and we liked it that way.

I'll never forget one year of particular abundance. I had collected so much candy that I wasn't sure what to do with all of it. I certainly wouldn't give any to my sister, who had collected about a tenth of what I had in my bulging, grocery sack full of goodies. That might set a precedent of goodwill that I would likely be expected to repeat in the future. I had worked hard for my candy, and I planned to keep every delectable morsel for myself. Faced with a dilemma of major proportions, I made the seemingly brilliant decision to be much like a pirate and bury my booty. So, I grabbed a healthy chunk of my candy, hermetically sealed it in a coffee can, and clandestinely buried it deep in the ground in our backyard, furtively looking from side to side to be certain I wasn't seen.

Six months later, when I was having a major case of sugar withdrawal, I suddenly remembered the buried hoard. I grabbed a shovel and excitedly dug up my treasure, only to discover that the can had somehow leaked, and what was once perfectly delicious candy was now moldy and rotten. I ate several pieces just to be sure, hoping beyond hope that at least some of the candy was still edible.

Sigh . . . no such luck.

I was depressed for weeks, but I learned from my experience that a child could never have too much candy at one time, and never again would I save it for the future.

∞∞∞

As I have become an adult, autumn is still my favorite season, but for different reasons. While I still have a sweet tooth of major proportions, it is a fraction of what it used to be. Nowadays, at least part of my love for autumn lies in the beauty of the surroundings. The kaleidoscope of colors, whether gold, brown, orange, red or yellow, strike me as being representative of God's multicolored palette, painting the environment in pleasant, soft, comforting hues. Also, autumn is the time for harvest, a gathering of the fruits of one's labors. As compared to spring and summer with their inherent frenetic activities, and winter, where survival from the cold is the prime directive, autumn is the ideal season to ask the questions: *What is the end result of the seeds I planted this year? What can I do better?*

In spite of my sugar craving, now my favorite holiday is Thanksgiving. As opposed to Christmas with its rampant commercialism and out-of-control gift giving, Thanksgiving is a time of expressing thanks for my many blessings, celebrated by a sumptuous meal with loved ones. No presents are expected or necessary, just good food, camaraderie, and conversation, not necessarily in that order. In short, I love the simplicity, love, and grace that come with autumn, the best time of year for just about everything. But, as I think about it, I wonder:

Are adults allowed to trick or treat?

Chapter Twenty-Five

Sleeping In As A Spiritual Practice

"The early bird gets the worm."

– Proverb

"Early to bed and early to rise makes a man healthy, wealthy, and wise."

– Benjamin Franklin

From long ago, a thick, suffocating layer of guilt has been imposed upon anyone who made the unfortunate decision to sleep in. No matter that you were up late the night before laboring around the house, or that you had worked your fingers to the bone over the preceding weeks at your stressful, screaming meemies job. The overall societal consensus was that if you didn't spring into action at the crack of dawn, you were assumed to be a lazy, indolent, good-for-nothing slouch who preferred to take it easy rather than put in an honest, hard day's work. Yes, in the eyes of Benjamin Franklin and his army of over-achievers, simply because you chose to loll in bed, you were destined for ill health, poverty, and poor decision making.

Against this background, just recently I had a hectic week in the emergency department, one with lots of difficult shifts. After completing that flurry of pressured activity, I went home and collapsed in my bed, exhausted. When I woke the next morning, I fought off Ben's admonition and, instead, made a conscious choice to stay in bed and relax. Lying there resting, a kaleidoscope of thoughts began to float across my mind, some from times past, others from the present, and some from an anticipated future. While a number were enjoyable, some were disturbing, others frightening, and some exhilarating.

Whatever their quality, I smiled at them and let them cycle through my consciousness until they lost their power and dissipated. I closed my eyes, once again fell into a deep slumber, and in moments visited Dreamland. As opposed to late-night dreams that are often forgotten, I clearly remembered those subconscious reflections when I woke a short time later. After examining the dreams, a totally different, unique set of thoughts greeted me, and once again, I dispassionately let them move in and out of my mind. Much like the classic Clint Eastwood movie, *The Good, the Bad and the Ugly*, they were what they were, and I did not attempt to control or judge them.

A short time later, though, I once again went to sleep, more dreams occurred, and the continuum of thoughts to dreams and dreams to thoughts went on for hours until, refreshed and relaxed, I stretched, rose from bed and engaged the day. Now, as I reflect on my experience, in many ways, this process was like a deep meditation, and much spiritual work had been accomplished.

As I ponder my morning of R & R, I believe our fast-paced culture is long overdue for a different mindset about the pleasures of sleeping in. In our driven, goal-oriented Western society, we sometimes forget the necessity of a balance between activity and passivity. In the East, this is best demonstrated in Taoism, where our dualistic world is represented by the Yin and the Yang, which together make up an indivisible whole. Good and bad, light and dark, wisdom and foolishness, day and night, truth and falsehoods, and yes, activity and passivity, all make up the dichotomy that is our Universe. In other words, one aspect doesn't exist without the other.

The long and the short of it is this: I vow to let go of the need to always be an early bird. No longer will I feel guilty about staying in bed and relaxing, or, in general, taking it easy, for not only will the extra rest do me good, but also healthy, sacred healing can take place. No, I don't plan to sleep in every day, but I will enjoy it to the fullest when I do so. After all, no matter what Benjamin Franklin said, I deserve to sleep in every so often and have some quiet moments to balance my oftentimes frenzied life.

Sleeping in *can* be a spiritual practice, don't you agree?

Chapter Twenty-Six

DANCERS

After a long, stressful day in the emergency department, nothing relaxes me more than going out to the pool and playing ball and water games with my dogs, Karma and Buddy. Once they are as exhausted as I am, I lie back in one of the lawn chairs and dry out, napping and bathing in the healing energy of the surrounding oak trees, floating white clouds above me, the twitter of birds, and the screech of Mississippi Kites as they circle overhead. Dragonflies are common visitors to the pool and often perform aerodynamic maneuvers over the water, flitting back and forth as if they are trying to entertain me. The atmosphere provides much-needed rejuvenation after facing the gut-wrenching travails of my work. Painful memories imprinted in my consciousness from my emergency shift dissipate as the warm embrace of my home environment enfolds me, and I find myself grateful.

One particular day, though, I had an unexpected visitor. As I slept by the pool, I was awakened by the feeling of a light tickling on my left leg, gently nudging me from my slumber. Opening my eyes, I glanced down at my knee and was delighted to discover a tiny praying mantis. As opposed to the adult it would become someday, this little insect was no more than dime-sized and had a light, translucent green color. The tiny bug was very delicate and fragile, and I was relieved that I didn't reflexively brush it off and injure the little creature.

Perhaps it was my imagination, but I felt certain that the praying mantis noticed that I was paying attention to it, and it began to crawl up my leg and onto my bathing suit. Every so often, it would stop, gaze at me with its tiny head, and sway back and forth, much like a Middle Eastern exotic dancer, with slow, seductive movements.

I was sure that the little insect was also very curious about me, and it continued to move up onto my stomach in jerky spurts. After a bit, it would stop and dance, rhythmically swaying back and forth. I quickly fell in love with my new friend and became enchanted by its delicate appearance as it moved up my arm onto my shoulder. I was not frightened in the least.

Hi, little guy! I thought as I smiled at it.

But then, to my great disappointment, it suddenly disappeared.

My praying mantis pal had vanished to parts unknown.

∞∞∞

Only a few days later, I had another "Close Encounter of the Insect Kind." As before, I was lounging in a lawn chair, dropping in and out of a light sleep, when, in a moment of hazy awareness, I noticed that one of the beautiful dragon-flies that frequented the pool had decided to say hello and perch on my right big toe. Perhaps it had seen how friendly I was to the little praying mantis and decided that it, too, would investigate the strange, sprawling giant of a creature.

I was spellbound and tried to hold as still as possible. I didn't want to startle the double-winged insect by any rapid movements. As it lingered, I was able to closely inspect it. The tail was a fluorescent, royal blue color with four segments bounded by small, black rings. The head had a slight greenish tinge to it, which appeared to be a shade of teal. No doubt the dragonfly was as interested in me as I was in it.

After we stared at each other for a while, I dozed off again, and when I awoke, the dragonfly was gone. I was disappointed, but moments later, it returned. This cycle of visitation and departure was repeated a number of times over the next thirty minutes or so, as the winged visitor danced off and on my toe, though sometimes it left for only a few seconds before returning. Like the praying mantis, I loved this dragonfly, and I know it felt the same about me. Finally, though, my new dragonfly friend decided that it had other, more serious things to do, and it flitted away, not to return.

∞∞∞

Just when I thought my interactions with the insect world couldn't get any better, one morning I was doing my usual lounging by the pool, and I noticed that a number of differently colored dragonflies were playing overhead. Much to my surprise, *two* of the lovely, aerodynamic wizards landed on my feet, this time on *both* of my big toes. I had the suspicion that they were a couple, at least for the time being, and they were a different color than the previous visitor, with their tails being a light-blue hue. I watched in delight as they flew on and off my toes, much like actors and actresses going on and off a stage. Like my previous moments with the royal blue dragonfly, they danced on and off my feet for a while before they left to explore the world.

In the days to come, I would be entertained by a butterfly that landed on my leg, one that looked like a brown oak leaf, and sometime later by a baby bumblebee that thought my hand was the perfect place to hang out.

How wonderful was that?

∞∞∞

As I reflect on these experiences, I feel joyful and connected with Mother Nature. Later, I realized that all of these events had two things in common. First, none of the insects were afraid of me, and second, we were curious about each other. I wanted to know as much about them as possible, and they seemed driven to learn about me as well.

I believe that the creatures of this Earth know when another wishes them harm, and I might guess that they sensed the nonviolence in my nature. Like most Buddhists, I believe in the sacredness of life and, if at all possible, not inflicting suffering on anything, whether it walks, crawls, swims, or flies. Obviously, there are exceptions to this rule, such as when a Buddhist monastery had to call an exterminator when their place was overrun by cockroaches. I do confess to eating fish occasionally. I suspect, though, that someday this habit will change.

Otherwise, I'm going to try to remain as harmless as possible to other forms of life. Who knows which others of God's creatures I might get to know?

Many, I hope.

Chapter Twenty-Seven

GOD

God is everywhere.
There's nowhere that He's not.
Whether lofty mountaintops,
Verdant forests,
Scorching deserts,
Frigid arctic ice fields,
Moon and stars,
Bottom of the sea,
Or busy city streets.
He is there.
Yet, there are times
When the pain of life becomes overwhelming,
Tears stream down my cheeks
And I cry out,
"Oh, God! Help me!"
His answer never comes in words
Rather, the wind on my face is His kiss.
The warming sun is His comforting embrace.

And the earth beneath my feet is His reassurance.
If I take the time to breathe
And look inside myself,
I also find Him in my heart,
Omnipresent, healing, loving,
Never apart from me,
Never apart from anyone,
God.

Chapter Twenty-Eight

LOVE NEVER DIES

My mother's death on August 12, 2016, followed years of suffering, primarily due to the arthritic discomfort of polymyalgia rheumatica, an inflammatory disease that caused her to have horrific, ongoing musculoskeletal pain. This devastating illness was complicated by multiple falls with subsequent fractures of her pelvis and ankle, and pain management only afforded her some modicum of relief. For me and the rest of the family, to witness the persistent misery she endured was agonizing beyond words.

As her health continued to deteriorate, we did all we could to let her know how much we loved her. As I mentioned in a previous blog post, we discovered that she was much comforted when old church songs were sung to her, such as *Amazing Grace, It is Well with My Soul, The Old Rugged Cross, How Great Thou Art,* among other Christian classics. Oftentimes, we would sing songs that she requested, but as she gradually became unresponsive, we simply sang those tunes that we knew she treasured. On occasion, we would detect a bit of a smile on her face, but toward the end, she gave no indication that she heard our voices. Only hours before Mom died, my sister, Connie, and I belted out a number of these melodies as we sat at her bedside. Such was our way of communicating with our dear mother, and we both believed that somehow she still heard these heartfelt renditions.

The funeral service some days later was well attended and lovely, though I knew the healing process would take a long time. I'm not sure, however, that anyone ever fully recovers from the death of a beloved parent. I suffered mightily in the beginning, realizing that my world was now topsy-turvy and had been forever changed. But, with the healing power of time, I learned to live with the vacuum created by my mother's death, and life went on simply because I had no other choice. Feeling a personal need to stay in touch, I made it a habit to occasionally talk with Mom and repeatedly tell her how much I loved her. While I never heard a response to these seemingly one-sided conversations, little did I know that one day the inexplicable would happen, and she would finally answer me in a way that still leaves me shaking my head in amazement.

∞∞∞

Over a year after mom's death, I was upstairs in my home office when I heard music coming from a room below. Knowing that my wife Sheridan was outside warming herself in front of a crackling fire in our chiminea, I wandered downstairs to see what was up. Much to my surprise, the television was on and playing old Christian music. My eyes welled with tears as I first heard *The Old Rugged Cross*, followed by *It is Well with My Soul,* and finally, *Amazing Grace.* My mother loved all of these tunes, and while I had no idea how she'd done it, I was confident that Sheridan had somehow programmed the television to broadcast those songs. I was deeply touched, and when Sheridan came in from outside, I thanked her for setting up the TV in that way. She looked confused at my words and said, "I didn't do anything."

"What?" I questioned, surprised.

"Gary," she compassionately repeated, seeing the baffled look on my face, "I didn't do anything. When I went outside, the TV was off. I never turned it on."

"But . . . how?" I asked.

"I don't know," Sheridan added, shrugging her shoulders.

I felt the blood drain from my face, and I stared at her in stupefaction.

This can't be, I thought.

I was so stunned by this surreal event that I couldn't bring myself to tell anyone. *How do I explain the impossible?* After all, somehow the television, along with the cable box, and the pre-amp, came on spontaneously, and besides that, the songs that sequentially played when I happened to arrive at the foot of the stairs were three of my mother's favorites.

Being a scientist at heart, I felt this had to be a random, serendipitous cosmic event, following the known rules of the Universe. But what would be the odds of such a happening without some kind of direction? While putting an exact number on the likelihood of this event occurring fortuitously would be impossible, the probability was certainly infinitesimally small.

Over the weeks to come, I felt overwhelmed by the implausibility of this occurrence. Finally, with no small amount of trepidation, but after enough time and the chance to think deeply about the episode, I shared this story with my sister, my father, and some of my friends. I was reluctant to tell others, concerned that they might believe I had finally gone off the deep end, traipsing into the world of insanity, wanting so badly to communicate with my mother that my mind played tricks on me. To my relief, I had selected well, and all responded with compassion and understanding, especially my father, who had no doubt whatsoever about the veracity of my story.

∞∞∞

Now, I am reminded of the words of Zen Master Thich Nhat Hanh, who once said, "No birth, no death, only transformation." In other words, we have always been and always will be. Birth and death are simply events of transition as we move in and out of manifestation on this Earth. So, with this in mind, I must ask *and* answer the following questions:

Does my mother still exist?

Unequivocally, yes.

With death, has the love disappeared that my mother and I shared?

Of course not.

Is death a barrier to communication with those we love?

Yes.

Is it possible for this barrier to be breached?

Yes. After my experience, how could I answer otherwise?

So, after much consideration, I have come to the inescapable conclusion that my mother whispered to me from beyond the grave, albeit in a most unique way. She let me know not only how much she enjoyed hearing these songs in her dying moments, but also that she lives on, and I am most grateful to have both of these understandings confirmed.

So, thank you, Mom, for reaching out to me. May your story give a measure of comfort to those who have doubts that their loved ones continue to exist. I am, and always will be, your son, even though the chasm of death separates us.

And that's a wonderful feeling.

I love you, Mom.

Chapter Twenty-Nine

HEALING TOUCH

Sometimes in the morning
And perhaps late at night,
Sheridan offers to rub my scalp and neck,
While we are lying in our bed.
I rest there as she caresses me,
My head resting on her chest.
In that moment,
Past, present, and future blend together
And time disappears.
Her warm fingers rhythmically dance across my head
Finding tender places
Ones that melt away with her touch.
I relax completely,
Intermittently dozing in the silence,
And I dream,
Random, unconnected scenes crossing my open mind.
When I wake,
I am aware of her comforting touch,

Rubbing away my hidden pain,
My deepest fears,
My anxieties,
My insecurities,
Buried deep within my mind.
And then I dream again,
Cycling between consciousness and unconsciousness.
I hold these moments as sacred,
Realizing that someday such pleasures will be in the
past.
But now, I find myself healing.
I sigh and let go.
I release my imperfections into the ethers,
For I know,
I am blessed,
And I am loved.

Chapter Thirty

DAMN THE TORPEDOES

Do you recall the days when you were young and the world was at your fingertips? Nothing, no *nothing* could get in your way, and any setbacks were only temporary. Death was an abstract concept, too far in the distance to worry or even consider. You effortlessly cavorted around your difficulties, much like a ballet dancer in perfect form. Nothing could stop you; you were Superboy or Supergirl, the strongest of the strong. You were untouchable and invincible, at least, that's how it seemed in the Pollyanna days.

Then, with time, inevitable chinks, dents, and tarnish began to appear in your shining, perfect armor. Maybe you found yourself in a job or home that was less than satisfying. Your Cinderella marriage, one you planned to stay in for life, perhaps had significant problems or even failed. Much to your chagrin, no fairy godmother materialized to wave her wand, pronounce the magic words "bibbidi bobbidi boo," and make it all okay again. Health issues start to reveal themselves, ones with no ready solutions. Loved ones fall away – no maybe about this one – death claiming those dearest to you, one by one, and the grim specter of your upcoming passing begins to look you directly in the eyes. The stark realization occurs that, unless you are Elijah of biblical fame, before long, it's curtains for you, and the only unanswered question is: *How bad will it be?* The "Golden Years" becomes a hollow jest, and with a start. you realize the joke's on you.

Pretty heavy, isn't it?

With all this in mind, just recently I had my sixty-fourth birthday. As I approach the Medicare and Social Security years, more than occasionally I think about the idealism of my youth, the hard lessons and growth experiences that life provided me, and the inevitability of death. Amazingly, though not surprisingly, perspective changes with increasing age. That said, unlike many in Western society who are revulsed by the idea of dying and decaying in the grave, I choose not to get too overly concerned about my eventual demise. Not that I wouldn't profoundly miss the day-to-day relationships with those I love and the pursuit of the joys that life offers, *certainly* I would. But I don't think of dying in a dark, morbid way, as our youth-obsessed culture seems to believe. Rather, I view it as a transition, a movement from one phase of existence into another.

When that fated time comes, I don't want to be as a pure, bright-eyed, cherubic youth, untouched by the experiences of life. Rather, I picture myself more as a gnarled, dead tree lying on the ground. Like the tree, the scars inflicted on me over the decades would show that I tried to engage life and live it as fully as possible, perhaps frightened at times, and maybe even scared out of my mind, but overall, willing to take chances.

Chief Tecumseh once wisely said, "When it comes your time to die, be not like those whose hearts are filled with the fear of death, so that when their time comes they weep and pray for a little more time to live their lives over again in a different way. Sing your death song and die like a hero going home."

If you live your life "all in," not perfectly, of course, no one can do that, death can be peaceful. You didn't stand to the side while conflict swirled all around you. You dove in headfirst, doing all you could to keep your head above the rising water, and to paraphrase Admiral David Farragut, you "damned the torpedoes and went full speed ahead." You may have been badly wounded as a result of your involvement, but whether you won or lost in the struggles of life isn't as important as the fact that you engaged them as completely as possible.

Embrace your battle scars; you've earned them. And if you do just that, when the time comes for you to make The Great Transition, you'll be able to sing your death song proudly.

After all, you'll have every right to do so.

Chapter Thirty-One

SEARCHING FOR GOD

I really want to see you
Really want to be with you
Really want to see you, Lord
But it takes so long, my Lord

From "My Sweet Lord," by George Harrison

Many years ago
I began sitting in meditation,
Listening inside,
Searching for God.
As I focused on my breath
Thoughts danced through my mind,
Begging for attention.
I slowly inhaled and exhaled
And released these reflections from the past.
Yet, unbidden they returned

Over and over again,
Unwelcome intruders,
Monkey mind.
Even now, when I quietly contemplate,
Distracting thoughts greet me
Clothed in different garments.
Yet sometimes – just sometimes,
I am able to gently brush them aside
And move my consciousness deep within myself
To a holy, sacred place.
I breathe deeply and abide there,
Feeling warm, nurtured, and comforted,
Much as a baby in his mother's womb,
And I am at peace.

Chapter Thirty-Two

THE WART

"All around us is a healing power, a life force that emanates from the sun, the air and the earth. Some call it *prana*, and some call it *chi*. Whatever, there are those who are naturally able to direct this energy into another person and help bring about balance and healing."
— Tiare Rapu, from *Murder at Stonehenge*

One of the ongoing issues of growing older is the springing forth of a seeming multitude of skin lesions. Most are innocuous, such as itchy moles of various shapes and sizes often discovered on your back in locations where you are unable to scratch them. In addition, irritating skin tags can emerge in an infinite number of places, sometimes catching on your clothes. Of course, the minute you have these skin blemishes removed at the dermatologist's office, invariably an entirely new host emerges to take their places, and you can almost hear them laughing as they say in a high-pitched chorus, "Aha! Thought you got rid of us, didn't you? Ha!"

Some can be serious, though, and should be caught early, such as pre-cancers and various malignant skin lesions frequently seen in sun-exposed areas. That's why I recommend everyone should be regularly examined by a dermatologist for routine screening and treatment if necessary.

This disclaimer aside, another relatively common skin lesion is the wart, which I remember being afflicted by off and on throughout my childhood years. Most eventually fell off on their own, though some hardier versions would require a trip to the dermatologist to have them frozen with liquid nitrogen, the staple of the skin doctor. To prevent them, of course, I followed the advice of every kid on the block and avoided picking up toads or frogs, which were sure to infect you with their spiny warts. Later I learned that was not true, in spite of the warty appearance of the little slimy amphibians. And thank God I never had a wart on my nose, or by definition, I would undoubtedly grow up to be a witch, or would I be a warlock?

As an adult, I can't recall the last time I had one of these pesky, irritating growths, until about – gulp – six months ago. At that time, I noticed one rearing its ugly, scaly head on the skin just inside my right eye adjacent to my nose. Surely, I thought, this lesion, with all the appearance of fetal cauliflower, would go away with time just like those of my youth. But this one fought off my hopes and prayers and only grew bigger and more annoying with every passing day. Since warts can be spread by scratching, it took all the willpower I had to keep my fingernails away from it. Fortunately, though, the little bugger didn't propagate and have baby warts. I wasn't fond of the idea of a wart family establishing a colony on my face, eventually growing into such a large conglomeration that I would look like the proverbial Elephant Man and be shunned by friends and family alike.

Research into this problem revealed that warts are caused by the human papillomavirus, transmitted by casual skin contact or through shared objects such as washcloths or towels. It has been estimated that around thirty percent of children will have warts, compared to three to five percent of adults. This is believed to be due to the more immature immune system of children, which becomes more adept at preventing warts as they grow older. Adults who have warts either have or have been suspected to have weakened immune systems.

What's wrong with my immunity? I wondered.

But I also discovered that most warts say *sayonara* in one to five years without any treatment. So, why worry?

That said, with time my disfiguring wart continued to grow along with my anxieties and self-consciousness. Thank God that my patients couldn't see the wart as it was mostly hidden behind the frames of my glasses. I then remembered that my colleague and mentor in integrative medicine, Dr. Andrew Weil, had recommended visualization therapy, and perhaps guided imagery and clinical hypnosis as possible therapies for warts. He once described a man who had used his particular interest in stream shovels to get rid of a wart by picturing a steam shovel scraping it out.

With this in mind, I discovered a most interesting book titled, *Remarkable Recovery: What Extraordinary Healings Tell Us About Getting Well and Staying Alive*, by Marc Ian Barasch and Caryle Hirshberg, the forward written by my friend, Dr. Larry Dossey. In the book, a rather remarkable experiment is described:

"The most notorious, most homely, and most medically unequivocal instance of the mind curing the body is the lowly wart. Generations of internists, dermatologists, and their wise grandmothers have known these blemishes, tough as box turtles, can be mentally zapped out of existence if the patient can be induced to believe. In one study reported by Dr. Lewis Thomas, fourteen patients literally covered with the growths were hypnotized and told that the warts on one side of their bodies would go away. Within a few weeks, all or nearly all the warts on that side of their bodies disappeared. The warts on the other side flourished as brazenly as ever."

Can you imagine participating in such an experiment, and later wondering what you were going to do about the warts on the other side? Talk about imbalanced!

So, I was convinced. Why not try visualization to heal my troublesome wart? I decided to concoct my own experiment. While I believed the steam shovel idea was interesting, how much better would the visualization be if I chose something that I truly believed in, rather than some arbitrary idea conjured up just for the sake of removing the pesky growth. That said, for as long as I can remember, I have felt certain that the energy of the Universe surrounds us at all times, simply waiting to be directed to heal and rejuvenate us. While there was no guarantee of success, why couldn't it work with me? It might, and it was worth a shot. After all, as the book by M. Scott Peck is titled, I preferred *The Road Less Traveled*.

And so I began. Several times a day, I would sit quietly, close my eyes, and visualize pure, scintillating golden light flowing from above me into the crown of my head. From there, I directed the light down my neck and into one arm, sometimes the right, sometimes the left, and then into the respective hand and index finger. I pictured the light being fiery hot, much like a hot iron poker. Sometimes I visualized my index finger as white hot, and other times as flaming red.

Once prepared, I placed my index finger on the wart, applying gentle pressure, imagining a sizzling sound and smoke rising from the burned lesion as it melted away, spiritually cauterized. I kept my finger on it, moving in slow circles, making sure that no part of the wart had been missed. After a few minutes, I pulled my finger away, satisfied that my work had been accomplished

I must confess that for the first few weeks, I had a lot of confidence and perhaps a bit of hubris that my technique would work. After all, wasn't my approach more imaginative, more dexterous, and more inspired than a steam shovel? The weeks passed into a month, then to months, and after three to four months of working on this visualization daily, my exuberance began to wane. Doubts began to occur, and I started to wonder if I was playing a fool's game. I found myself practicing my technique less and less. My wart became more noticeable and bothersome, and I began dreaming of a trip to the dermatologist's office, where liquid nitrogen in the hands of a skilled practitioner would take away this lingering nightmare. But this was during the time of the coronavirus pandemic, and several phone calls to different offices had the same result:

"I'm sorry, sir. Our office is closed for now. Would you like to do a virtual visit with the doctor?"

Fat chance that will help, I thought as I politely said, "Okay, I'll get back with you later." I thought I would likely go insane before Covid-19 waned enough to make an appointment.

And then it happened: I had a short dream that the scaly enigma, the wart, had fallen off my face into my hand. *Is it possible*, I wondered? *Is my intuitive self trying to encourage me? Was victory right around the corner?*

Energized, I renewed my visualizations, perhaps with not so much vigor and excitement, but I patiently went through the steps all the same. About a month later, my persistence was rewarded. I woke up one morning and discovered that the wart was gone, nowhere to be found.

∞ ∞ ∞

Now, in retrospect, it's hard to imagine that a simple wart would cause me so much consternation. While I truly believe in the power of the mind and the ability we all have to direct healing energy, for the longest time the wart resisted, as if it were trying to test me. And maybe it was. While I don't necessarily feel proud that I was nearly beaten into submission by a humble skin lesion, I'm happy that I kept after it.

In all fairness, perhaps the wart would have gone away on its own without any intervention whatsoever. While the scientist in me believes that is possible, in my heart and soul, I think that the spiritual work I did made a difference. Maybe next time when I get a wart, I'll just wait and watch and see what happens. Perhaps tincture of time is all that was required.

Then again, maybe not.

Chapter Thirty-Three

THE LEADER OF THE BAND

The leader of the band is tired and
his eyes are growing old
But his blood runs through my instrument and
his song is in my soul
My life has been a poor attempt to imitate the man
I'm just a living legacy to the leader of the band
– Dan Fogelberg

I first met Jerry Lavender in the spring of 1994. At that difficult time, I was still battered and bruised from a painful divorce that had occurred in the latter part of '92, and I was in the process of rediscovering myself. *Who am I? What am I? Why do I hurt so much? What did I do to deserve this? Where do I go from here?* Intensely introspective, I sought out anything that might make me feel semi-human again, anything that might ease the grief I was feeling. In the midst of my search, I recalled how much joy I had previously experienced with singing. I was raised in the

Methodist church, and I had sung in the choir from grade school through the summers of my college days.

Several of those moments stood out to me. I was but a young boy in elementary school when my church choir director asked me to sing a solo. Not being one who enjoyed standing up in front of others to perform, at first I resisted, but eventually I came around to her way of thinking. For some reason, God knows why, I chose not to say a word about the upcoming momentous event to my parents. A few weeks later, I stood up in my light blue choir robe and sang "In the Garden" at the Sunday morning church service. I still remember the shocked looks on my parents' faces and how my mother wept throughout the performance.

Another fond memory occurred some years later when I sang in the adult church choir. One of my buddies in the group was Richard Moody, a white-haired senior who enjoyed singing and laughing at least as much as I did. A song we both particularly liked was the Christian classic, "'Tis Marvelous and Wonderful," and one day Richard was at my family's home doing handyman work in the garage, and we decided to seize the opportunity. As I sang tenor, Richard sang bass, and we cut loose with a rousing two-part version of that joyous melody. After a few stanzas, though, we heard howling, much like that of a wounded, rabid dog, and we discovered my brother Jim had been listening outside and had concluded that he couldn't take our somewhat less-than-melodious rendition anymore.

With this history in mind, I decided to check around and see if I could find a community chorus where I could sing. To my delight, I discovered the Edmond Community Chorale (ECC), a group that met weekly on the campus of the University of Central Oklahoma. Fighting back my apprehension, I decided to give it a try and give my love of music an opportunity to heal me.

∞∞∞

I'll never forget the first time I walked into choir practice. Around fifty to sixty people were in the room, some standing, some sitting as they chatted before the rehearsal began. At the front stood the director, Dr. Lon Dehnert, who warmly greeted me and introduced me to the pianist, Dr. Ron Wallace. Then Lon led me to the tenor section, where I first met Jerry, a pleasant, balding man in his early sixties with a bright smile and a good-natured way about him. I liked him immediately, and after a few moments of conversation, the choir began the vocal warm ups. Shortly afterward, we were given our music for the semester, the glorious Handel's *Messiah*.

And so began my twenty-four-year friendship with Jerry. Every Tuesday night, during the spring and fall school semesters, we would meet, converse, and sing our hearts out, with Jerry always seated to my left. The more I sang with him, the more I realized what a fine tenor he was. Without fail, he would hit the pitches and rhythms perfectly, and he rarely missed an entrance. When I was uncertain about how our tenor part went, all I had to do was listen to Jerry, and I was always on solid ground.

∞∞∞

Oh, what glorious music we sang over the years! Besides *Messiah*, my personal favorites included Haydn's *Creation*, Mozart's *Requiem*, Vivaldi's *Gloria,* and Brahms' *A*

German Requiem. With time, my musical skills gradually improved, and my friendship with Jerry deepened. On occasion, he would ask me to join him for a duet at his church, Olivet Baptist, in northwest Oklahoma City. After a practice or two, we would sing a song for his Sunday school class, and while all of our performances were well received, the clear favorite over the years was the bouncy, toe-tapping spiritual by Aaron Copland, "Ching a Ring Chaw."

Around four years ago, Jerry left ECC, saying that he needed to care for his wife, who had been chronically ill for years. While I understood his situation, I felt as if my heart had been ripped from my chest. After all, I had heard his voice in my left ear for more than two decades. Last year, when one of our fellow ECC members passed away, Jerry rejoined the choir for a musical tribute at her funeral. How wonderful it was to be with him again, but little did I know that precious occasion would be the last time I would see him. My dear friend, Jerry Melvin Lavender, died on February 20, 2018, at eighty-five years of age.

∞∞∞

Now, as I think about Jerry, many warm thoughts come to mind. While he was a great tenor, he was a better friend. The Dalai Lama once said, "My religion is kindness," and Jerry was one of the kindest men I have ever known. Through all those years of our friendship, I never heard him say a bad word about anyone. Not only that, in spite of his conservative religious outlook, Jerry often told me how much he enjoyed the spiritually liberal books I had authored. Because he was my friend, not only did he tolerate my perspective, he embraced it, which was a great gift to me.

The world will not be the same without Jerry Lavender. When I heard of his death, my eyes welled with tears, yet after a short period of intense grieving, I realized how grateful I was that I had known him. I absolutely have no doubt that my years spent singing with him helped me eventually to heal from my wounds, and for that, I will forever be indebted to him. Besides, Jerry was a man who loved singing nearly as much as he loved life, so when he left the Chorale to provide for his wife, he made a tremendous personal sacrifice. But that's the way Jerry was; he always put others before himself.

I have often said that Jerry was the spiritual leader of the tenor section, and no doubt he was also a leader in our ECC "band." Today, much of what I am musically can be attributed to him, and I am honored to be part of Jerry's living legacy.

Isaac Newton once said, "If I have seen further than others, it is by standing upon the shoulders of giants." Jerry was one such giant, a man whose greatness was measured by living in a humble, giving, accepting, and loving manner.

I will miss him greatly.

Chapter Thirty-Four

THE CHOCOLATE CHIP COOKIE

"Think what a better world it would be if we all, the
whole world, had cookies and milk about three o'clock every
afternoon and then lay down on our blankets for a nap."
– Barbara Jordan

No one in the world bakes better chocolate chip
cookies than my wife, Sheridan. No one. I realize this sounds
a bit pretentious and grandiose, but it's not an exaggeration.
As the crusty Western actor Walter Brennan used to say in his
distinctive drawl, "No brag, just fact." Not only does Sheridan
prepare the cookies with the skill of a Cordon Bleu-trained
French pastry chef, at the same time, she infuses her bakery
creations with her own special ingredient – love. Not only is
the taste fabulous, but I also feel better, inside and out, after
sampling one.

They're that good.

On a particularly rough day, when I was slugging it

out in the emergency department, I received an e-mail from Sheridan informing me that she had prepared a fresh batch. Any difficulties I was having at the time vaporized into the ethers. For no matter how bad the chaos was, and, as might be expected, it was far worse than bad, in a few short hours I would be experiencing the nirvanic ecstasy of biting into one of her delectable cookies.

When I arrived home that evening, I quickly raced to the kitchen and over to the plate of cookies waiting for me on the countertop, surveyed the batch for the largest one and gobbled it down.

Amazing!

The next morning, as I was preparing to go to the gym for a workout, I grabbed two more and greedily consumed them as I rushed out the door. The crispy treat was just the boost I needed to start my morning.

Later, though, as I thought about it, I realized that while I had enjoyed the cookies immensely, I had to confess that I had been preoccupied with other matters while eating them. I was reminded of the words of Zen Buddhist master Thich Nhat Hanh, who once said, "Mindful eating means simply eating or drinking while being aware of each bite or sip."

When I recognized that I had not been attentively savoring these delicious cookies, I made the decision that in the evening, I would give my full attention and awareness to this sacred, gustatory experience.

As the sunlight waned, with great anticipation I mindfully walked to the kitchen, where the plate of tantalizing goodies sat on the countertop and beckoned to me. First, I picked up one, turned it in my hand and gazed at it. The cookie was light-brown and crispy, sprinkled with chocolate chips and packed with loads of pecans. As I took my first bite and slowly chewed, allowing the crunchy goodness to melt in my mouth, I breathed in and out and began to think deeply about what the cookie truly consisted of. First of all, the pecans in it were native to Oklahoma, arguably the best in the world. Carefully cultivated near the small Oklahoma community of Earlsboro, they were a loving present from my father, who always gifted bags of them to us at Christmas. The cocoa and vanilla likely originated in rainy, equatorial countries, as they grow well in humid, tropical climates. The eggs came from cage-free chickens that were organically fed, literally "Happy Eggs" from fowl that roamed the country-side, scratched the ground, and ate bugs and worms. The butter, also organic, came from cows that were free of poten-tially dangerous chemicals and hormones. Most of the ingre-dients of Sheridan's cookies required timely rainwater for their eventual production, and besides that, the sun, along with the fertile earth, were necessary for the healthy growth of the cocoa and pecan trees, vanilla plants, sugar cane, and wheat.

So, what does one of Sheridan's chocolate chip cook-ies actually contain? When I take a bite, in addition to the healthy ingredients, I am absorbing the essence of the warm, comforting sun, billowing rain clouds, the nurturing earth, the vigilance and attentiveness of the farmer, the caring of my father, and, of course, the love of my wife. The cookie provides so much more than just a snack. Like many foods prepared with love and mindfulness, this chocolate chip cookie is a gift from God and is as holy and hallowed as a sacramental wafer at the ritual of communion.

I smile in gratitude as I humbly accept this blessing. Thank you, Sheridan.

Chapter Thirty-Five

THE TIME PORTAL

I have many vivid memories of growing up in my childhood home. As described in my book, *Oklahoma Is Where I Live,* probably one of the strongest was when a tornado ravaged our modest house, blowing the roof off while my family cowered in my sister's small bedroom.

While everything else falls far short of that cataclysmic event, I still recall the multicolored pepper plants situated in the flower bed out front, and how once I thought I'd try a taste of one. They were meant to be strictly ornamental, but I felt as though my mouth was on fire as I dashed into the house for water, believing fluids would help, but of course, they didn't. And how could I forget Snappy and Mandy, our terrier mixes, who produced numerous litters of cute, squirmy, licking puppies? God, I loved our dogs, furry, loving little creatures that provided such joy and unconditional love.

One distinctive feature of the home that still vividly stands out in my mind, even after more than five decades, was a framed picture that hung in our dining room. In the painting, a peasant man and woman stood alone in a cultivated field at the end of the day, their heads bowed in prayer. On the ground between the pair was what appeared to be a basket of potatoes. To the man's right, a pitchfork was firmly planted in the ground, while behind the woman rested a primitive wheelbarrow. In the far distance, a barely visible church steeple peeked up from the cloudy horizon.

As Dad was a farmer, when I was a boy I asked him what the painting meant to him. As I recall, he said that the humility of the couple and their modest surroundings reminded him of his farmer roots in Davidson, Oklahoma, and how challenging life was when he was a youth. Also, with the God's help, somehow the farmers got by, which meant a lot to Dad.

Later, I discovered that this reproduction was called *The Angelus* and was painted by the French artist, Jean-François Millet, completed between 1857 and 1859. The Angelus, a Catholic devotion commemorating the incarnation of Jesus Christ, and as the title indicated, was the prayer the couple was reciting that marked the end of their day's work.

When my parents eventually moved to another home, the painting graced their bedroom, but I will always remember it being in our dining room, the symbolic centerpiece of our family in my childhood.

∞∞∞

Paris has often been called "The City of Love," and until my wife Sheridan introduced me to the place, I had no idea precisely what that meant. Now, though, after visiting, at least I have some idea of the inherent romance imbued in the city. Impossible to describe in words, an energy saturates the city with a feeling of excitement, framed and showcased by ancient history. Besides world-class museums, the culinary scene is like none other in the world. In addition, nothing compares with the joy of walking down a bustling Paris street, and the sights, sounds, and aromas create an ambiance totally unique to Paris, one that exists nowhere else in the world.

As a footnote, rumor has it that Parisians are stuffy and unfriendly, but that was certainly not my experience. Instead, as long as a visitor tries to communicate some in French (after all – you *are* in France) and simply start every conversation with a hearty *Bonjour!* before speaking English, this will set the interaction on the right path toward a smooth encounter. Besides, it helps to say *s'il vous plaît* and *merci* every now and then. As one might guess, it's best not to have a disrespectful "Ugly American,"—"I'm better than you are" – sort of attitude.

All this said, our three-day far-too-short sashay into Paris took place after making an exploratory trip into the UK to visit England and Wales to do research for my then-upcoming book, *Murder at Stonehenge*. That completed, from London we took an approximately two and a half hour high-speed Eurostar train ride through the Chunnel to Paris.

And what a trip it was! We stayed at a centrally located hotel not far from the Louvre, and we were right in the middle of all the action. We crammed as much activity as possible into our abbreviated vacation, taking a visit to the Eiffel Tower, with a one-of-a-kind breathtaking view of the Seine River as it wound through the city. We also participated in a guided tour of the Louvre, where we gazed upon many eye-popping works of art, including the Regent Diamond, an over one-hundred forty carat stone having an estimated worth of over seventy-five million dollars, and generally felt to be the most beautiful diamond in the world. Two magnificent Johannes Vermeer pieces, *The Astronomer* and *The Lacemaker,* were next on the tour. Later that same day, we attended a wine tasting at a nearby bistro.

Ooh la la!

On another afternoon, we adventured to the Paris Flea Market. *Flea Market?* I can almost hear you thinking. Actually, this is nothing like the ratty stateside flea markets with piles of wanted and unwanted junk. Rather, it's the largest of its kind in the world and is literally packed with antique treasures. On a typical weekend, it receives anywhere from 120,000 to 180,000 visitors each day. Pretty amazing, huh?

Unexpected lightning struck on the day we visited the *Musée D'Orsay,* within walking distance from our hotel just across the Seine. Sheridan and I had already spent hours *oohing* and *aahing* at the magnificent collection of art, when all of a sudden, there it was, a painting of a peasant couple bowing their heads in a field at dusk. I couldn't believe my eyes and caught my breath.

The Millet painting.

The Angelus.

Oh my God.

I was completely caught off guard, stunned by seeing the original painting in person, so different from the reproduction at my childhood home. I could see the brushstrokes of the artist and almost feel his passion as he painted the scene. I was flooded with emotion as I one-pointedly gazed at it, and all sorts of images from the past opened up before me in rapid sequence. In my mind, many long-forgotten memories swirling before me:

Our family, Mom, Dad, brother Jim, sister Connie, and I, like the painting, praying before we ate our meals.

My pigeon coop in the southeast corner of the backyard, lovingly built for me by my father.

The Christmas when my parents gave me my first guitar. Little did they know at the time how powerfully this present would affect me.

Intense, maniacal, gut-wrenching ping pong games with Jim in the garage – how we both hated to lose!

My gerbils, Willard and Cathy, running amok on the living room sofa. Can you believe how tolerant my parents were?

Birthday celebrations, too numerous to count. The more friends I invited, the more presents, right?

Getting up early every morning to deliver the *Daily Oklahoman* newspaper. On Sundays, after dispensing the heavy and bulky Sunday edition, Dad always took Jim and me out to the local donut shop for fresh, warm, melt-in-your-mouth donuts.

The tetherball pole in the backyard. Because we played regularly at home, Jim, Connie, and I were nearly undefeatable at school.

My purple, high-powered softball bat.

The time when I tearfully went to my coach's home and quit my elementary school baseball team, the Hillcrest Hornets.

Most important of all, I had an overpowering feeling of being loved. I was safe, protected, and cared for, something every child should be imbued with.

∞∞∞

In the months that followed the powerful experience of seeing Millet's *Angelus*, other recollections from that time have unexpectedly sprung forth, several worth mentioning.

One thing I clearly recall was the emotional trauma brought about by the game of Wahoo. This board game became so popular in the '60s that families were creating their own unique homemade versions. Wahoo was a cutthroat game that invariably brought out the worst in people, their screaming, insulting, aggressive side. Our board was made by one of our neighbors, and while we would occasionally play the game in the family, the main knock-down, drag-out, take-no-prisoners version occurred when my Dad and Mom would go down the road to Norman to play with my Uncle Dale and Aunt Reba. We kids would generally stay with a babysitter for these competitions, and invariably Dad and Mom would return home with ruffled feathers and arguing with each other. Mom would always complain that Dad and Uncle Dale had a "warped sense of humor," and we all noticed that communications between Mom and Dad over the following week or so were limited and tense.

Now, if I ever wondered where my somewhat perverse humor came from, I had to look no further than my Dad on the day he proudly arrived at home with a rubber hot dog in hand. In my way of thinking, this was the greatest invention since buttered bread, and much to my surprise, Mom seemed to be as excited about the idea as we were. We waited with great anticipation for our first victim to arrive. Before long, the blessed event occurred when our family friend, Charles, came to our house, thinking he get some good home-cooked food. I still recall Jim, Connie, and I snickering and fighting back the urge to laugh out loud as Mom served up the hot dogs, the rubber one going to our guest. She expectantly said, "Eat up!"

While I don't recall the exact words, I feel certain that after Charles took a big bite of his chili, relish, and mustard-coated rubber hot dog, his face turned beet red and he said something to the effect of, "What the Hell?" We all burst out laughing at that point, and Charles knew he had been the brunt of one of our family jokes. Of course, then Mom served him a real hot dog with all the trimmings, not another rubber frankfurter. Wouldn't it have been great if we'd had a second one?

Speaking of humor, it was sad but true that the favorite place in our middle-class neighborhood for cats in heat to gather and mate was in the bushes beneath Dad and Mom's bedroom window. Of course, this exalted experience always occurred in the deep of night, and after hearing numerous males fighting it out over the females, and the cats collectively meowing in ecstasy – with a sound much like that of a baby crying – in the morning Mom would emerge from the bedroom droopy-eyed with a sleepy, angry look on her face. She invariably said, "I've been up all night listening to those damned cats." These were the only times I heard my mother curse, and as you might guess, cats never were allowed to become a part of our family.

Another memory comes from when the youth from our church would have a gathering at my home for some social time together. I vividly remember the first song I fast-danced to, titled *Little Girl* by the Syndicate of Sound. By nature, I was and still am – believe it or not -- an introvert, so dancing in front of others with a girl, no less, was quite a leap for me. I still recall the opening lines of the song:

Hey, little girl, you don't have to hide
nothin' no more

You didn't do nothin' that hadn't been done before
Little girl thought she wouldn't get caught, you see
She thought she'd get away with goin' out
on me, yeah.

The song was a toe-tapper, and the tune is firmly implanted in my memory.

∞∞∞

Looking back, while the trip to Paris was no doubt one of the most wonderful experiences of my life, the one sacred event of seeing the original Millet painting, *The Angelus*, stood out. Someday, Sheridan and I will return to Paris, and once again, I'll revisit the time portal that cracked open the safe that secured the precious memories of my youth.

And who knows what new recollections will spring forth.

Chapter Thirty-Six

GUILT

"Abraham," Matt interrupted, "I feel . . . I feel so terribly guilty for the things I've done."

My son," Abraham said, "guilt is a useful feeling; it makes you aware of a wrongful doing. There its purpose ends. When one feels guilt, one should try to correct the misdeed, and if unable to do so, ask forgiveness of the one you have wronged. If for some reason even that is not possible, direct your plea to God, and there your responsibility ends."

From *The Lhasa Trilogy*

Guilt is one of the most pervasive emotions in our society, and sometimes I wonder why. Certainly, the roots for many of us come from our childhood, as many parents unfortunately use guilt as a tactic to manipulate their children. I believe that at least some of you have heard phases similar to these during your early years: "You're a bad boy if you don't study hard." "If you don't eat all of your food on the plate, you're a bad girl. Starving children all over the world would love to trade places with you."

Ouch!

In addition, all of us have grab bags of situations in which we wish we had made different decisions. Of course, I've had my share. Some of them have floated around in my psyche, making me wince as I recalled them, as if I'm being stung repeatedly by a swarm of angry hornets. No matter that the actions that have caused these painful recollections are long over and done with, they hurt, and they hurt badly, reminding me that intellectual understanding is entirely different from visceral.

So, what to do?

Years ago, my wife Sheridan and I were in Sri Lanka, enjoying a vacation together while I was also collecting material for a new book. We spent several days in Tangalle on the southern coast, kicking back and resting on the beach, enjoying the warm, pleasant weather and the rhythmic, healing sound of the crashing waves. Feeling relaxed and at peace, I breathed deeply and let the restorative energy of the sea wash through my consciousness. Fully embracing the moment, I mentally repeated:

"Breathing in, I feel the healing of the ocean bathing my heart and soul. Breathing out, I am healed."

After a while, something remarkable happened. Inner psychic pain that I had held within myself for a long, long time gradually began to dissipate. I felt soothed and comforted, and, oddly enough, lighter, as if a millstone had been removed from around my neck.

The spiritual experience I had while in Sri Lanka can happen with any of us, and a beach is not necessary. All you need is a place that feels comforting, whether in a garden, a quiet room, the woods, the desert, sitting before a picture of a saint, or anywhere that produces an atmosphere of peace and relaxation. Also required is a willingness to accept your humanness, realizing that no one gets it right all the time. I some-how suspect – as hard as it may be for some of you to believe – that even Jesus had moments when he fell short of perfection. Think Joseph and Mary might have been grounded him for sneaking kisses from the girls at the synagogue? Or maybe for cheating on his final exam in carpentry? Or perhaps when he got caught in the wee hours in the garden of Gethsemane drinking wine and telling dirty jokes with his friends?

On a more serious note, you also must be ready to let the Divine, whoever or whatever that is for you, ease your guilt away, dissolving it into the ethers, never to be seen or heard from again. However you choose to release the shame, regret, or remorse you're holding onto, it's a worthwhile endeavor to do so. If you've learned your lessons from previous missteps, guilt is no longer necessary – it's of no use to you whatsoever.

When you have some quiet time, give this exercise a try. You might be surprised by how much better and lighter you will feel without that burdensome millstone around your neck.

Chapter Thirty-Seven

SPRINGTIME

As the radiant sun
Breaks through wispy clouds,
I hear warm wind whooshing through the trees,
Branches dancing to and fro.
Twittering birds flit about,
Building nests for tiny eggs.
Blessed beads around my neck
Speak to me of holy times.
Dogs smiling as I pet them,
Eyes aglow with love.
I feel my heart open
As I see green leaves bursting forth.
The energy is building,
Fresh, vibrant, effervescent, hopeful.
The Phoenix is born
From the ashes of the Earth.
Springtime is here.

Chapter Thirty-Eight

MEMORIES OF A DISTANT TIME

Sometimes I sit back and recall the past when I was a naïve young boy observing the world around me. The differences between then and now are stark and stretch the limits of one's imagination, but isn't that true for all from generation to generation? Now, at the ripe old age of sixty-seven, at long last, I understand why the elders have traditionally sat and pondered the times of their youth, longing for the comfort and security of those moments when they were growing up, generally free of responsibilities.

In my way of thinking, the most striking difference between then and now has been the many advancements of technology. The Internet did not exist in my childhood and only became widely used in the mid-1990s. So, any research that had to be done took place in libraries, painstakingly looking up journal articles and hoping they were available there. If not, one had to utilize an interlibrary loan to get the needed information, which could take days or even weeks. No "Googling" existed to discover obscure facts within seconds.

Also, as hard as it is to believe in this day and age, cell phones did not come into widespread public use until the mid-1980s, and at that time, they were just phones, not multifunctional smartphones that worked as computers at your fingertips. In my medical school and internship days, we carried beepers when we needed to be notified by nursing staff. Once the little bugger went off, we would scurry to a nearby phone, sometimes a phone booth if we were out and about, and call the number displayed. Nowadays, beepers are mostly a thing of the past.

Speaking of technology, I still recall the day when all televisions were black and white. When color TVs came out, only the wealthiest families could afford them. When one of our neighbors bought a color TV, we all had to pay a visit to take a gander. Imagine our disappointment at the poor quality of the image. Later, the picture would get a lot better, but at the time, the television screen looked more like black and white with a tinge of color. Not so great, but eventually all of us had a color television in order to keep up with the neighbors. For my family, that took some time.

As a child, the monarch butterfly migrations in fall and spring were always memorable. I'll never forget those occasions in grade school, when we kids would go outside for recess and see the sky flooded with these amazing winged insects making their biannual three-thousand-mile journey to warmer climes in Mexico. I would dance with them as they flitted across the playground, lovely creatures that were much hardier than their delicate multicolored appearance would indicate. If anything suggested the presence of God in the world, this incredible phenomenon certainly did.

Sadly enough, in modern times, these migrations are

a mere whisper of what they used to be. The overall numbers of Monarchs have dropped by more than eighty percent over the past twenty years. Why is that? Evidence would suggest – no surprise here – that humans are the cause. Climate change, with the subsequent increase in carbon dioxide levels, makes milkweed, the only food monarchs can eat, too toxic for ingestion. Besides that, with the evolution of herbicide-resistant corn, farmers can spray without discretion to eliminate weeds that compete with their crops, one of which is milkweed. Also, higher temperatures are forcing the monarch butterflies' breeding areas ever farther north, making their migration much longer and more challenging. I long for those Days of the Monarch, but now it seems that the time for this twice-yearly miracle has passed. I feel sad, not only for the butterflies, but also for future generations who will likely never see such a spectacular event.

Another creature I fondly remember from days past is the Texas horned lizard, also known as the horny toad. It was not uncommon for us to find these cute, spiky creatures as we prowled around the playground at school. Looking much like miniature dinosaurs, once we caught them, we would turn them over on their backs and rub their tummies. After a few moments, they appeared to fall asleep. Now, in retrospect, I'm not certain whether they were napping or lying there paralyzed in fear. Regardless, now the population of the official state reptile of Texas has plummeted and has been declared threatened. The reasons for this precipitous decline include habitat encroachment, climate change (sound familiar?), the deleterious effect of pesticides on the horny toad's primary food source, the harvester ant, as well as on the reptiles themselves. As a child, I loved the horny toad, and I still do, though nowadays they are nowhere to be found.

Today, as I think about it, I am amazed that any of us from the older generation survived childhood. Any one of a number of things could, and perhaps should, have gone wrong. In particular, I recall the fascination and seductiveness of the liquid metal, mercury. At least occasionally, a kid would show up with a small vial of the stuff at school. They never explained how they got it, though a common source was from a thermometer that they broke just to get a sample. Our favorite thing to do with the liquid was to coat our silver coins with it. It was remarkable how much more beautiful they looked with their new silvery finish, and we were near-ecstatic to see them brightly shine.

Fortunately, elemental mercury is poorly absorbed through the skin, and its toxic effect occurs when the vapors are inhaled, which mainly occurs when it's heated. While I doubt that any right-minded person would sit around and sniff heated mercury, absorption *can* occur if a mercury spill is cleaned up with a vacuum cleaner. The bottom line is this: mercury is a heavy metal in the same family of cadmium, lead, and arsenic, and exposure at any level is not healthy. Indeed, the phrase "Mad as a Hatter" is thought to be due to the toxic effects of mercury poisoning on workers in the old hat-making industry. But we were kids. What did we know?

Another ill-considered pastime of childhood not conducive to wellness was the ability to make each other pass out. I'll never forget the day when one of my classmates claimed that he could make us bite the dust. I watched as the scene unfolded, which went something like this.

A large boy named Butch boasted, "Hey! I can make any of you faint. Do you believe me?"

A crowd of kids gathered round, and Edwin, a scrawny red-haired kid, walked up from the back of the group and said, "No way!"

Flexing his muscles, Butch said, "I dare you to let me try. Well?"

Looking a little nervous, Edwin said, "Well . . . okay."

With that, Butch walked behind him, wrapped his arms around Edwin's chest and ordered, "Breathe hard and fast. In a few minutes, I want you to take a deep breath and bear down."

Doing as instructed, at the moment Edwin stopped breathing and bore down, Butch squeezed his chest in a bear hug. A second later, Edwin dropped to the ground, passed out cold, his head loudly thudding against the rock-hard playground dirt.

I couldn't believe it. Surely he couldn't do the same thing to me. After all, I was a lot tougher than Edwin.

"Hey Butch," I confidently said. "I'll bet you can't do that with me."

Butch said, "We'll see about that!"

Butch had an evil grin on his face as he walked behind me and repeated the same instructions that he gave to Edwin.

As I bore down and felt his strong arms around me, I fought hard to stay conscious, but all to no avail. I roughly crumpled down unconscious, abruptly realizing that mind over matter did not work in this situation. I later understood that hyperventilation, followed by chest squeezing, stimulated the vagus nerve, producing a slow heart rate and subsequent syncope. Fortunately, no lasting damage was done. I didn't hit my head or sustain a neck injury, but I somehow managed to escape what could have easily become a catastrophe.

Back in the olden days, treating illness was not as scientific as it generally is currently, and many a time, I recall being on the receiving end of dubious home remedies that had been passed down through generations to my mother. One particular treatment that I particularly hated was taking aspirin. No, I don't mean swallowing the pills whole; I mean *sucking* on them. My dear mother believed that when I or my siblings had a sore throat, the best use of aspirin was to put it directly where the pain was. I still recall the bitter, acrid taste of adult aspirin, not the more tolerable baby aspirin, as it dissolved in my young, sensitive throat. *Ugh!* The end result of this torturous treatment was that I learned never to complain of a sore throat, for I knew what the awful remedy would be.

Another treatment that I hated was applied when I had a cough and congestion. True to the questionable theory that Mom used with aspirin, I was often given the abhorrent mixture of *Vicks VapoRub* with sugar to take *by mouth*. Yes, as hard as it is to believe, I was instructed to swallow it. While such a small amount is not harmful if used on the skin, the ingredients camphor, menthol, oil of eucalyptus, turpentine oil, among other nasty chemicals, are not meant for internal use. Old wives' tales seem to be especially powerful to young mothers desperate for treatments to soothe their children, and mine was no exception.

∞∞∞

It's funny to me how such memories from childhood can remain lodged in your consciousness. Much like a satisfying meal, they can stick to your ribs, especially compared to the current times. In all likelihood, the youth growing up in our society today will have similar recollections of ridiculous medical practices used on them by their parents. As Bob Dylan once prophetically sang, *The Times They Are A-Changin.'*

That said, I can only pray that by taking the right steps to protect our environment, once again magnificent swarms of monarch butterflies will return to be viewed with awe, horny toads can be found again in your suburban backyards, and home remedies will not be quite so intrusive and potentially dangerous. I somehow suspect, though, that kids will continue to make each other pass out, and even more likely, find a way to get mercury to play with.

It's just too much fun.

Chapter Thirty-Nine

RAIN

If the rain comes
They run and hide their heads
They might as well be dead
If the rain comes
If the rain comes
From "Rain," by The Beatles

"Truly I say to you, except you be converted
and become as little children, you shall
not enter into the kingdom of heaven."
– Matthew 18:3

To my delight, when I awoke this morning, I discovered a gentle, drizzling rain was falling. The precipitation was light, so I couldn't hear the raindrops sprinkling on the roof as I lay in bed, but when I looked out the window, I saw the rain dancing on the surface of the swimming pool and on the concrete patio behind my home. Later, when I walked outside to retrieve the newspaper, the air was crisp, fresh, and cool. To me, nothing smells quite as good as the refreshing aroma during and after a rain.

A kaleidoscope of thoughts crossed my mind, but the first was how rain nurtures the land. During my childhood, my family lived on a forty-acre farm near Dickson, Oklahoma. Years later, my father leased farmland south of Oklahoma City, where he cultivated wheat, cotton, soybeans, and grain sorghum, none of which was irrigated. When Dad was a youngster growing up in Davidson, the success of his family's crops was likewise completely dependent on precipitation. Given that droughts in Oklahoma occur more than occasionally, I still recall the look of relief on my father's face when we had a pleasant, soaking rain, and almost overnight his cultivated fields turned from a dull, brownish-green to verdant hues sparkling with life. Rain was truly manna from heaven for those who tilled the earth, and was absolutely critical for sustenance and survival. Besides that, to older generations of Oklahoma farmers, the lack of rain no doubt brought up visceral, unpleasant recollections of the misery of the Dust Bowl.

A good rain also brings up fond memories from my childhood. As long as there was no associated lightning, my mother allowed me, my brother, Jim, and sister, Connie, to put on our bathing suits and frolic outside in the rain. Often we were joined by our neighborhood chums and any others who dared hang around with a wild, playful group of kids. The more torrential the rain was, the better, as when the streets flooded, we could wade, giggling and laughing, into the deep water and splash each other to our hearts' content.

As I grew older and allegedly more dignified, I shunned such childish activities. When the rains came, like

The Beatles described in the lyrics of the song above, I would ensconce myself within dry and cozy surroundings, and if I was required to venture outside, I would cover up as much as possible. After all, if I became cold and wet, couldn't I get sick? Become deathly ill with pneumonia? Staying shielded from the elements was safe and secure, and I thought this was the mature, adult way to behave.

Over the years, though, I have slowly regressed to some of my childhood ways. For example, my work as an emergency physician can be onerous, painful, and sometimes overwhelming. To lighten my emotional load, I have developed a somewhat childish, cornball sense of humor, one that my fellow healthcare workers have gradually come to tolerate and, on occasion, even embrace.

When the rain comes, though, there are no holds barred, and my adult completely disappears as my spontaneous inner child becomes unleashed. If it's warm enough, I put on my bathing suit, go outside by the pool and gleefully laugh as I feel this miraculous gift from God cleansing and purifying me from top to bottom. I joyfully re-enter the magical world of my childhood, one where I was deeply loved by my parents and community of friends, and my universe was effervescent, innocent, and pure.

While there are times when I am still required to be a responsible adult, fortunately moments occur when I can be that carefree, happy boy of earlier years. While being a sensible adult is important in the proper setting, sometimes I prefer to return to the child I was in years past. After all, Jesus said I must be as a little child to enter the kingdom of heaven.

All in all, I believe I'm making progress.

Chapter Forty

DEAFENING

One day, while in the middle of the devastating coronavirus pandemic of 2020, I was laboring in the emergency department when one of the nurses approached me with a small piece of white paper in her hand.

Glancing down at it, she said, "Emergency Medical Services is bringing in a cardiac arrest. ETA is ten minutes."

"What's the story?"

"Thirty-two year old –

Oh, no, I thought.

"— with a history of asthma. He started having trouble breathing last night, and this morning he became unresponsive. EMS found him pulseless and in asystole – flatline. He's been intubated and given IV epinephrine and nebulized Albuterol through his endotracheal tube. He has had no response."

My heart sank. I knew that asthmatics who go into cardiac arrest are very unlikely to be resuscitated, but we would do the very best that we could to save him.

∞∞∞

I was in the room with the nursing staff when the patient was wheeled into the room. "Any change in status?" I asked the paramedic.

"None."

"Still in asystole?"

"Yes."

"How long has he been down?"

"CPR was done at the scene by the family for around five minutes prior to our arrival, and we've been working the patient for . . ." she looked at her watch . . . "around thirty more minutes."

"Meds?"

"To this point, he has had six milligrams of epinephrine IV, and I just gave him two amps of bicarb." She glanced at me with a sad look in her eyes. "As I said, he's had no improvement."

By this time, the patient had been unloaded from the ambulance stretcher onto the emergency department gurney, and I focused my full attention on him. He appeared close to his stated age and was in cardiac arrest. His pupils were fixed and dilated, and an endotracheal tube, a breathing tube, was in place in his throat. He had no cardiac sounds, and his lungs were tight, extremely difficult to ventilate, and with each breath, expiratory wheezing was heard. The rest of his exam revealed nothing remarkable.

I knew the young man was dead, but I couldn't stop our efforts. Not yet. He was too young; there was so much more of life for him to experience, but I already knew he wouldn't. We continued our work with him for a while longer, and when I was finally certain that nothing else could

be done to bring him back to the land of the living, I pro-
nounced him dead.

∞∞∞

Shortly after his death, I asked the nursing staff to col-
lect a coronavirus screen. I wondered if that was the reason
for his precipitous decline, but the results came back negative. In the meantime, after I took a few moments to gather
my wits, it was time to break the terrible news to the family
who had arrived a short time ago.

As his chart was handed to me, I glanced at his name –
Bryce Williams. The nursing staff told me that the patient's
mother and two sisters were waiting, and understandably,
they were anxious to hear any news. I braced myself. This
would not be easy.

Chart in hand, I slowly walked into the family room,
where the family awaited. I cleared my throat and said, "I'm
very sorry to tell you this --"

With these few words, all started moaning, the sound
of their voices gradually rising to a crescendo, accompanied
by looks of fear in their eyes.

"— but Bryce is dead."

At that point, all three family members began screaming wildly at the tops of their lungs, the sisters thrashing and
bouncing from wall to wall across the small room. I side-
stepped one of them, who in her anxiety barely missed col-
liding with me.

The sound was deafening, and with the sudden as-
sault of noise, for a moment I felt shocked and disoriented.
*Who am I? Where was I? Why was I here? What the holy hell
just happened?*

As I recovered from my daze, I tried to communicate with the family, but they were so caught up in their grief that they could not comprehend what I had to say. The mother wailed over and over again, "I want to see my son."

I repeatedly explained, "I'm sorry, but you can't. With the pandemic, no family is allowed in the emergency department. It's just not safe."

The mother ignored my repeated explanations, and I certainly understood. I wanted her to see her dead son too, but I couldn't let her enter. The nursing staff stayed close at hand and comforted the family as best they could.

I walked back to my desk in the emergency department and sat down, still in somewhat of a stupor, saddened by the circumstances of what had just occurred. Later, when the family was ready, I would confer with them and gather further details, Information I needed before speaking to the medical examiner.

∞∞∞

So much fear has been generated by the coronavirus, and rightfully so. The average death rate in America is around 1.7 percent, seventeen per thousand. Because this virus is a newcomer to the world, there is practically no immunity, and it can rapidly spread through the populace unabated. At the time of this writing, almost eighty-six million have been infected worldwide, and more than twenty-one million have come from the United States. By the time we have a vaccine, there will be many more; the only question is how many will be added to the burgeoning list.

The haunting image that still lingers with me is that of the young man's mother, pleading with me and the nursing staff to see the body of her newly-dead son. Never in my forty-two-year career in emergency medicine have I been forced to refuse to let someone have closure with one they loved, and I can only imagine how I might react in a similar situation.

But such is the inhumanity the coronavirus has forced upon us. Because of this blight, we have been required to adopt necessary but inhumane behaviors that challenge our concepts of acceptable and reasonable conduct.

Also imprinted on my mind is the piercing, overwhelming wall of sound produced by those grieving family members. I am reminded of how everyone's reaction to death is different. Some are quiet in their suffering, while others can be loud and animated. I never judge how people react, but rather, I try to be sympathetic with their unique expressions of grief.

Over all these years, I have seen a number of people die, some who had already passed away before reaching me, and many whom my dedicated nursing staff and I tried desperately to save, but to no avail. While death is not unusual in my line of work, losses that are easiest to deal with emotionally are those who pass away at a ripe old age. The ones that rip at my heart and soul are those who die unexpectedly in their youthful years. Over my long career, some cases have been imbedded deep within my psyche, the pain of those experiences only fading with the passage of time. Because of the unusual circumstances, this one, the far-too-early death of Bryce Williams, will hang in my consciousness for a while.

A very long while . . .

Chapter Forty-One

MIRACULOUS

Throughout my career in emergency medicine, certain cases stand out, such as "The Asthma Attack," mentioned in my book, *The Pit*. Most of the time, however, emergency department health care providers troll in the commonplace, such as recurrent abdominal pain, shortness of breath, chronic back pain, lacerations, fevers, overdoses, this and that, over and over again. This monotonous repetition has a tendency to make physicians sleepwalk and put them in a near-comatose state of redundancy. But longevity in my work has taught me never to take anything at face value.

Some patients, though, who come through the doors of the emergency department, look so critically ill at the onset that the physician has no doubt that something life-threatening is occurring. By continually reassessing the situation and knowing that one's initial impressions may not be entirely accurate, a correct diagnosis can be made. Also, certain cases make the physician look beyond the *milieu* of commonality. As is often said, when one hears hoofbeats, one should eventually see a horse gallop around the corner. But every so often, much to everyone's surprise, a zebra comes into view.

In my over forty-two years as an emergency physician, I have never seen such as case as this one. Yes, she was a zebra straight from the Tanzanian Serengeti. Interestingly enough, as hard as it may be to believe, I had a similar case the following year, though with an entirely different presentation. They say in emergency medicine that cases come in threes. When will the next one pop into the emergency department? Whenever, I'll be ready for it.

At least, I hope I am.

∞∞∞

On Tuesday morning, September 25th, 2018, I was laboring in the emergency department, and while I was doing some charting at my desk, I was approached by one of the RNs.

"Dr. Conrad," she said, "We have a very ill-appearing thirty-year- old white female in room eleven complaining of chest and abdominal pain."

"I'll see her right now."

When I walked into the room, I knew something was terribly wrong. Patients her age shouldn't look this sick. She was very pale, sweaty and appeared dusky. *Yes,* I thought to myself, *whatever is ailing her, this young lady is seriously ill.* The nursing staff was already in the room, starting an IV and drawing blood. Likewise, they knew something was amiss. In the big scheme of things, I am certain that quick-acting nurses have saved far more patients' lives than doctors.

A man with a deeply concerned look on his face stood

at her side. He was stocky, well over six feet tall, and had brown hair with a matching beard and moustache. He wore a red baseball cap with black lettering on the front.

"Tell me what's going on," I asked.

He spoke first. "Hi, I'm her husband, Lance, and this is my wife Audery."

"Nice to meet both of you," I said, nodding my head. "Go on."

Audery said, "Last night, while I was working at the casino, I stopped for a moment to have my lunch break and eat a taco. I was about a quarter of the way through when it began to taste funny."

"Did you think the food was bad?" I asked.

"Yes," she answered. "Obviously, I stopped eating, but later I had severe chest pain, and I felt like a three hundred pound man was sitting on my chest. I was short of breath, and my stomach hurt badly. I have asthma, so I tried my inhaler."

"Did it help?"

"Not really."

"What happened next?"

"My co-workers in the break room saw that I was sick, so they notified the security guard, who took me to an office and called for an ambulance. He also phoned Lance, who arrived shortly after the ambulance personnel. I was then taken to a hospital."

"Not this one?"

"No."

"Okay. What occurred there?"

Lance chimed in. "Once she got there, she started having severe vomiting and diarrhea. They did a number of tests, and they were all negative. They said she had food poisoning and that her chest pain was caused by indigestion. They sent her home."

I couldn't help but wonder if she looked this sick at the other hospital. I had to guess not. No emergency physician worth his or her salt would send a patient home who looked as bad as she did, no matter what the test results showed.

"What happened after that?"

"I was up and down all night with vomiting and diarrhea. I felt horrible."

"What made you come to see me this morning?

Lance spoke again. "I was up with her most of the night, as I'd decided to stay home from work to take care of her. I was dozing when I was awakened by a loud, crashing sound. I found that Audery had fallen from the bed and onto the floor. Her skin was a sickly blue color; her eyes were empty of life and stared straight ahead. She was not breathing or responding, and I thought she was dead. I felt a weak pulse, though, so I gave her artificial respiration, which seemed to help. She started to breathe again, but she was still unconscious and made gurgling sounds. When the ambulance arrived, she was groaning and saying words that were indecipherable. The paramedic found her blood pressure was 96/58. An IV was started, she was placed on oxygen, and they left with lights and sirens to go to the hospital."

"That must have been very frightening." I asked Audery, "When was your last menstrual period?"

"I'm on it right now."

"Any surgeries?"

"I've had my gallbladder taken out, and I've had a tubal ligation."

"Anything else?" I asked.

"No," she answered.

I glanced at the vital signs on her chart. Her blood pressure had dropped even further to 69/51, the pulse rate was extremely high at 143, and she had no temperature. Her respiratory rate and oxygen saturation were normal. The physical exam revealed a white female in moderate distress. Her conjunctivae – the mucous membranes that line the inner surface of the eyelids – were pink, leading me to believe that her low blood pressure was not from blood loss. Other than a rapid heart rate, her heart and lungs sounded normal. She had diffuse lower abdominal tenderness, which was not exquisite, and her extremity exam was unremarkable.

What's going on? I questioned myself. *Is she septic, with bacteria in her bloodstream? Does she have pneumonia? A urinary tract infection? A perforation in her abdomen?* I was utterly baffled, but I knew without a doubt that I had to discover the cause of her distress as quickly as possible.

Because of her high heart rate and low blood pressure, an infusion of a large bolus of saline was administered. When that failed to help, a vasopressor – medication that helps increase blood pressure – was started, which resulted in modest improvement.

Her initial screening laboratory tests were worrisome. Her white blood count was over 25,000, far above the normal range, which made me suspect an overwhelming infection. Her lactic acid, a marker for sepsis, was markedly elevated. Antibiotics were started. The d-dimer, a marker of blood clots as well as sepsis, was also very high. While her EKG showed nothing exceptional except for a rapid heart rate, the chest x-ray was suspicious for free air under her left diaphragm, reinforcing my concern about a perforation. While the diagnostic possibilities were endless, given the x-ray findings, I felt the best test to do next was a CAT scan of the abdomen and pelvis.

Just as Audery was being urgently wheeled to x-ray, from around the corner, Megan and Meghan, two RNs I worked with in the emergency department, approached me.

"Doctor Conrad?"

"Yes?"

Meghan said, "We're both concerned about the patient in room eleven. We think that she might have an aneurysm."

Megan nodded. "Yes, we do."

I paused and thought carefully before I spoke. "I so appreciate your idea. No doubt something serious is going on, but I believe it's more likely she is septic, though I am uncertain of the cause."

They both nodded, and Megan said, "We both felt it was important to share our thoughts with you."

"Thank you. I'll let you know when we figure this out."

They smiled and walked away, but their words stuck in my mind. *Could they be right? Is this actually an aneurysm?* Over my years in emergency medicine, I've learned to listen to the nurses and never disregard their opinions. When we work together trying to piece together difficult cases, I'm positive that patient outcomes are better.

Moments later, the scan was completed, and the radiologist reported that Audery had inflammatory stranding – indicating a possible infection in her abdomen – but no perforation. Also, she had a large pericardial effusion, a collection of fluid around her heart. *What the hell? Why would she have that?* With a start, I suspected that the nurses were once again right. Audery likely had an aneurysm. I immediately ordered a STAT echocardiogram and asked the hospital operator to contact the cardiologist on call. The echo tech arrived promptly, and shortly after that, I had a diagnosis.

To my dismay, I discovered that Audery had a type A dissecting aneurysm of the aortic arch. In this case, the dissection involved a tear in the ascending part of the aorta, just as it branches off the heart. The associated mortality rate is a little over 30% for this condition. I had to act quickly; there was no time to lose.

Answering my call, the cardiologist immediately came to the emergency department with one of his colleagues to assist with the case. When I discovered that OU Medical Center was on divert, the cardiologist arranged a transfer to another facility with the capability to repair such a challenging problem. After Audery and Lance were informed of the gravity of the situation, Audery bravely said to her husband, "It'll be okay. I'll be fine."

Shortly thereafter, emergency medical services arrived and transported the patient to the referral hospital. I prayed that she would get there in time to save her young life. For the time being, though, I had to direct my attention to the other patients in my care. I had done all that I could for Audery, and I hoped that would be enough.

∞∞∞

The next day, I called to inquire about Audery's condition, and I was told that while she had survived the surgery, shortly after her chest was opened, the aneurysm had ruptured, and it took over twenty minutes to restore her blood flow. *What sort of damage would she sustain from such an insult?*

In the days that followed, Audery developed paralysis

of her right side and went into acute kidney failure. Later her paralysis resolved, and temporarily she required renal dialysis. Three weeks after her surgery, she was discharged to go for rehabilitation, where it was anticipated she would be for two to four weeks. After only a week of therapy, this amazingly strong woman had progressed so much she was able to be discharged home.

∞∞∞

Now, after over two and a half years since this dramatic case, I found myself wanting to know more details about the young woman's miraculous recovery, so I reached out to her and her husband with the hope of learning more. They readily agreed, and following are their personal recollections of this incredible experience.

First, Lance's statement:

"After I heard the news from Dr. Conrad that my wife had a life-threatening aneurysm, I broke down in tears. My brother, Mike, who had arrived at the hospital, hugged me and told me Audery was going to get through this. He said, 'She's too damn stubborn to die or leave you and the girls.' [Audery and Lance had two children, Amelia, nine years old, and Lily, six years old] I took a moment to steel myself, and then I notified both of our mothers as well as her boss before I went back into her room. Soon, as the ambulance prepared to leave, I kissed Audery, told her that I loved her, and that I would be there when she woke up from surgery.

"Mike and I drove to the referral hospital, and upon arrival, the staff placed us in the waiting area, and we were told her surgery had already begun. Soon, all sorts of friends and family showed up, and we had a veritable army of support. After an hour or so into the surgery, we were informed that Audery had crashed, but she had been resuscitated, and the surgery was underway.

"After several hours, I was out of my mind with worry and fear when the thoracic surgeon came to talk with us. He told us that as soon after they had opened her chest, the aneurysm ruptured, and it took some time to get the heart and lung machine attached. They were able to successfully revive her, though, and complete the surgery. He said that there was no way to know at that time what kind of damage had occurred while she was in cardiac arrest. They would keep her core temperature low and would do all they could to help her maintain brain function, but the odds of her survival were very low, and even if she did wake up she might have brain damage and memory loss. They told us that it would be about two to three hours before they would have her out of surgery.

"When Audery was finally in her room, I went in to see her, desperate for proof that she was still on the earth with me. Not knowing what to expect, I found my beautiful, strong, stubborn wife lying in a bed covered in ice packs and IVs in her arms. She had a breathing tube in her throat, and even if she wanted to talk, I knew she couldn't. I touched her foot and said, 'I'm right here, my love. I'll always be here. I love you.' While she gave no indication that she heard my words, I hoped that she could. I kissed my fingers and touched her foot. I thought: *She's alive, and I'll do everything I can to help her through this*. I felt so grateful, tears came to my eyes, and I turned around and thanked everyone in the room.

"The next day, the thoracic surgeon asked me to come with him and look at her MRI. He told me she had suffered extensive multi-organ damage and several strokes during her cardiac arrest, and he warned me that she might not have any memory of her family.

"In the days that followed, I stewed on the knowledge that the love of my life, my soul mate, might not remember me or our children. I'd have recurrent nightmares about that possibility, and I'd wake up crying and shaking. When that happened, I'd get up and go to her hospital room and sit with her, holding her hand, and singing our wedding song. I'd tell her how much the kids and I loved her.

"On the fourth day after her surgery, the surgeon and his assistant entered Audery's room and asked if I would step out so they could evaluate her. After I left the room, I heard them saying through the door, 'Audery, can you hear us? Can you wake up for us?'

"I immediately knew that this was a critical point. I paced outside the room, worrying, trembling, and praying. In the next few minutes, my world would either be saved or turned upside down.

"A few moments later, they came out of the room. The surgeon said she was responding, and that she would blink her eyes once for 'yes' and twice for 'no.' They told me I could speak to her if I wanted. I paused before I entered, trying to deal with the explosion of thoughts, feelings, and emotions.

"I finally walked in and stood beside her. I touched her hand and said 'Audery, this is Lance, your husband. Baby, can you wake up and look at me?' Her eyes fluttered open and focused on my face.

"I asked, 'Audery, do you recognize me?' She slowly blinked her eyes 'yes.' I took out my phone and pulled up a picture of one of the girls. 'Do you know who this is?' Again, she blinked 'yes.' I told her, 'I love you so much baby. We are all here for you.'

"The surgeon interrupted. 'It's time to let her rest.' After I left the room, I doubled over and started crying. I couldn't have felt more grateful and relieved.

"In the days that followed, her caregivers discovered that Audery had numbness and weakness of her right side. Physical therapy worked hard with her, and over the next couple of days, she improved. She was eventually able to have her breathing tube removed, she began eating, she could whisper and talk quietly, and her right foot and arm started to improve. I can't explain in words how ecstatically happy we were.

"Toward the end of the first week after surgery, Audery and I were watching TV when she squeezed my hand. She leaned over and whispered, 'What happened?' I could clearly see on her face the worry, confusion, fear, anger, and longing to know. That indescribable look still haunts me to this day. I told her everything I knew in the best detail I could. She sat there and listened, her eyes welling with tears.

"The next morning, I talked to the surgeon about the baby steps Audery was taking, and he shook his head and said, 'She's not taking baby steps; she's taking kangaroo leaps. We've never seen anything like this before. I have other patients with similar procedures, who, after months, made nowhere near the progress Audery is making. Keep up the good work!'

"Everyone at the hospital seemed to be aware of Audery's success story. It was amazing. People would shake her hand, high-five her and tell her what a great job she was doing in her recovery. But something lit a fire in Audery, and she wanted to progress even faster. She wanted to be able to walk, come home, and lie in bed with me.

"With a lot of effort on her part, by the end of the second week, she was walking with assistance, eating without diet restrictions and using her right hand and leg more and more. She could also talk with far less difficulty. On the third week, she was moved to a different room, and the staff started to prepare us to go to rehabilitation. Once there, she progressed so fast she was released after only a week. She came home exactly one month after her surgery, and she returned to work two months later.

"As I think about it, this situation was terrifying and horrific, but at the same time, beautifully miraculous. Audery is the strongest, most stubborn woman I know, and I truly am the luckiest man in the world to have found and have married such an amazing woman. Thank you, all of the doctors and nurses that all worked together to save my soul mate. If any one thing had gone wrong or was off by even a minute, Audery, my wife, the mother of my children, and my soul mate, could have died.

"There were so many cogs in the wheel of this machine that worked together to save her. I give myself some credit for resuscitating her and calling for help. I am deeply grateful to the ambulance personnel for responding so quickly and efficiently, Dr. Conrad for laboring so hard to figure out what was wrong with her, the cardiologists who worked with him and helped get her transferred to another facility, and, of course, the thoracic surgeon and all the physicians and nurses at the referral hospital.

"Most of all, I want to thank Audery for being strong and stubborn enough to survive this catastrophic problem. Without her, my universe would have been forever changed. I am so grateful to each and every one of you for this chain of miracles that kept her alive."

Audery's recollections:

"When someone first lays eyes on me, most don't see anything other than the exposed part of my scar that runs from the center of my chest to the hollow of my throat. Sometimes they see the other scars, like the ones on my arms and neck. I choose to show them openly and yes, sometimes I get looks of pity. But, also, I get looks of wonder, amazement, and admiration. My husband has told me, 'You should be proud of those scars. They are testaments to your story, one of strength and determination that begs to be told.' So, to anyone with 'battle scars,' as my husband affectionately calls them, do not hide them. Show them with pride. If you happen to see people with their scars out in the open, you might ask them about it, and you just might hear a life-changing story, one like mine.

"As you know from reading Dr. Conrad's and Lance's recollections, I became ill on the night of Monday, September 24th, while I was at work. The emergency department that I went to diagnosed me with food poisoning, and I was sent home.

"The next morning, at about 9:15 a.m., I felt I was going to get sick again. I sat up on the edge of the bed, and after I stood up to go to the bathroom, I passed out. My husband thought I had died.

"But I hadn't. The next thing I saw was the smiling face of my Grandma, who died some time ago. In the beginning, I was not aware of where I was, but soon I realized that I was at her country home near Sparks, Oklahoma, and we were both sitting on her yellow porch swing. We sat for a while watching the sunset, then I lay down with my head in her lap, and she played with my hair, much as she did when

I was a little girl.

"As I gazed straight ahead, I saw that the sun cut beautiful patterns of myriad shapes and colors through the tree branches at the edge of her yard. My Grandma looked every bit the same as I remembered, her sandy brown hair tinged with grey, wearing the same wire-framed glasses and the oh-so-familiar scent of White Diamonds perfume. I felt comfortable, warm, and secure.

"My dear Grandma looked lovingly at me and said, 'It's time for you to go back. You have to keep fighting and never give up." She stood up and gave me a kiss on my forehead, and turned to go back inside her home. She said, 'I'll always be watching.' God, how I loved my Grandma!

"For the next couple of days, it seemed as if I was trapped in a weird, altered state of consciousness. I felt like I was sitting strapped to a chair in a pitch-black room, unable to move or speak. Then I began to hear voices, first unfamiliar, then familiar ones, and all of a sudden, my surroundings shifted, and I felt I was traveling through a slide projector of pictures and different scenes of my life. Sometimes I'd hear music, and the flashes eventually took the shapes of my husband, kids, and pets. It was unbelievably scary, and no matter how much I wanted to ask what was going on, I just couldn't. I needed those flashes, though, like I needed air to breathe, and I would panic when I was not able to wake up and embrace them. I was so frustrated, then everything would suddenly go quiet, and I'd both settle down and get even more frightened at the same time. Sounds bizarre, doesn't it? But that's the way it was. Deep inside, I knew what I needed. I was desperate to wake up and see my husband and find out what happened to me.

"Once I finally woke up, I didn't want to go back to

sleep. I was afraid to. Every time I did, I'd have crazy dreams and wake up calling for my husband, who was nearly always sitting there beside me. Sometimes I'd have one of those dreams, and he would try to get me to calm down, telling me it was just a dream. I'd get mad and start yelling at him until I finally fell asleep, just to repeat the same process in another hour or so, over and over again. My husband never griped about this; he just continued to wake up and take care of me. He was so patient. We just laugh about it now.

"One thing I was sure of; I wanted to get home with my family. To do so, I knew that first I had to relearn how to talk, eat, bathe, brush my hair, write and walk again. There was so much that I couldn't do, and I didn't really understand why. I was both angry and scared, but at the same time, I was determined. Four weeks after my surgery, I went home. I was so happy, and my family was too!

"Now that I've settled into my life again, I have a bit of advice for those of you who have loved ones who go into a coma. Most importantly, don't give up on them. We can still hear you. We just can't respond because our reality is warped. We need you to talk, read, and sing to us, even if it's not directly to us. We can still hear you, and your communication gives us something to hold onto, a lifeline that we can grasp and pull ourselves back to reality. I can tell you from my own experience that if had it not been for my family, and *especially* my husband, Lance, I would most likely still be lost in a world of unreality, or even worse. I can't thank them enough.

"Still, every so often, I have chest pains with shortness of breath that come and go and feel like a hot poker stabbing me. I also have a seizure disorder because of the strokes I suffered, but they are well controlled with medication.

Considering what the alternative was, it's not a problem to deal with these issues. Besides that, I've been told that it's not a matter of if my aorta will give out, but a matter of when. So, knowing this, I try to spend each day with my family and loved ones. living my life to the fullest. I'm living proof that miracles can happen, so if you become critically ill, never lose hope and keep fighting.

"In conclusion, I want to say thank you to all of the doctors, nurses, physician associates, paramedics, and EMTs. For without every single one of you, I wouldn't be here today."

∞∞∞

I find myself greatly touched by the personal renditions of Audery and Lance. The in-depth discussion of their thoughts and feelings during their shared experience is unlike anything I've ever read in any medical text. Their words are unique, open, honest, and sometimes terrifying.

As I think deeply about Audery's recovery, one keyword keeps repeating itself: *teamwork*. As Lance so well described, if any one of the medical professionals had failed in his or her duty, Audery's life would have tipped over the edge and cascaded downward much like the water at Niagara Falls. But no one did. Everyone performed as was required, and as a result, Audery is alive.

Hats off to the paramedics and EMTs that first picked her up from her workplace, and later as they transported her from my hospital to the next, and kudos to the nursing staff at all of the institutions. They were responsible for skillfully starting her IVs, drawing blood, keeping close track of her vital signs, and being co-managers with the physicians. I'm not embarrassed in the least that the nurses at my hospital guessed the diagnosis before I did, as I'm a firm believer in nurses' intuition. What their guts tell them is usually correct, oftentimes well before physicians have a clue, and I appreciate the fact that they felt comfortable enough to share their thoughts with me. No physician is an omniscient, omnipresent, and omnipotent God, as much as some would like to believe otherwise.

Thanks also to the laboratory and x-ray technicians who dutifully performed their jobs, though special mention should go to the echocardiology tech who rushed to the emergency department that day. I have worked with him for years, and knowing the urgency, he dropped what he was doing and promptly answered the call. Shortly after he placed the probe on Audery's chest, he knew the diagnosis well before the cardiologist had a chance to look at the study, giving me a head start on getting Audery safely transferred.

And, of course, the physicians involved in Audery's case had something to do with her successful outcome. At my hospital, the team of an emergency physician, two cardiologists, and a radiologist labored together and formed an indefatigable network of physicians whose unified goal was to help Audery. Combined with everyone else at my facility, they bought her precious minutes until the thoracic surgeon could later perform the life-saving procedure.

Now that we've covered the mechanics of Audery's recovery, perhaps we should take a moment to discuss the spiritual aspects. In my mind, there is no doubt whatsoever that the love of her husband and family played a major role in her survival. What if Lance had not been in her room, singing to her, talking to her, letting her know she was loved, in order to help draw her from her unconscious state back to the world of the living?

And what about her Grandma, whose words of encouragement echoed through Audrey's consciousness during her desperate moments? Some believe that such visitations are hallucinations to a vulnerable mind, but I'm not one of them. I feel certain her Grandma was aware of her granddaughter's predicament and wanted to help in any way she could. I believe such otherworldly events such as this one are much more common than are reported, and those we love stay connected with us, whether they exist in this life or in the life to come.

I am honored that I was the physician who saw and treated Audery that fateful day. Her case will be one that I will always remember. The fact that a young woman still lives and is enjoying time with her husband and two small children, and that I am at least partially responsible for that, warms my heart.

God bless you, Audery. May your life be long and full of wonderful memories. After all you and your family have been through, you deserve it.

About The Author

Gary D. Conrad lives with his wife, Sheridan, and their dogs, Karma and Buddy, in Edmond, Oklahoma. Gary is an emergency and integrative physician, and his interests include Tibetan rights, meditation, the music of Joseph Haydn, choral work, and wilderness hiking.

Gary received his undergraduate diploma from Oklahoma State University, his M.D. degree from the University of Oklahoma. After finishing his internship in 1978, he has been a practitioner of emergency medicine in the greater Oklahoma City area. He has also completed a fellowship in integrative medicine at the University of Arizona.

Gary is the award-winning author of *The Lhasa Trilogy*, *Oklahoma Is Where I Live: and Other Things on My Mind*, *Murder on Easter Island: A Daniel 'Hawk' Fishinghawk Mystery*, *Murder at Stonehenge: A Daniel 'Hawk' Fishinghawk Mystery*, and *The Pit: Memoir of an Emergency Physician*.

Gary can be reached through his website at GaryDConrad.com.

Made in the USA
Columbia, SC
06 September 2021